EPITAPH

Paul Gittins

GREENSTONE
pictures

RANDOM
HOUSE
NEW ZEALAND LTD

Random House New Zealand Ltd
(An imprint of the Random House Group)

18 Poland Road
Glenfield
Auckland 10
NEW ZEALAND

Sydney   New York   Toronto
London   Auckland   Johannesburg
and agencies throughout the world

First published 1997

Cover photograph by Roberto Buzzolan
Photographs on title page and end page by Denene Marten, Greenstone Pictures
Where no source given, photographs by Greenstone Pictures

Printed in Wellington by GP Print
ISBN 1 86941 328 8

Contents

Acknowledgements

THIS BOOK WAS very much the result of a team effort. Researchers presented me with their research in the form of a personal journey which I then stepped into and made my own. During the making of the television series I became very familiar not only with those stories I researched myself, but with all the others as well, and have added any insights, intuitions or discoveries that came to me during this time. The researchers and the stories for which they are responsible are:

CAROLYN AVERY: The Waikino School Tragedy; "Love me, I am dying"; Oblivion; Love Letter; Against the Elements. TREVOR CONN: Caffrey and Penn; "Let them shoot me". MARK DERBY: Stiletto. MARK EVERTON: The Last Man Hanged. PAUL GITTINS: There is Nothing Covered That Shall Not Be Revealed; Over Niagara Falls; "My hands did not come upon that man". MARK McNEILL: The Confessions of a Cold-Blooded Killer. DENENE MARTEN: Broken Heart. KAREN SYDNEY: Te Rongopai a Ruka. MARY-JO TOHILL: Chinese Coffins; Somebody's Darling. Researching History's Mysteries, at the end of the book, was put together by Denene Marten and myself.

I am indebted to Harriet Allan of Random House who worked hard and long helping me shape and overwrite these stories so that they ring out with a single voice.

I would also like to thank Ruth Hamilton, Consultant to TVNZ Enterprises, for her encouragement in this project and for asking me to be involved; and John Harris of Greenstone Pictures for his help in coordinating the book and for his support.

Thanks to the many institutions that provided invaluable assistance to our researchers: the Family Research Centre in Auckland Central City Library; the Auckland Museum Library; the National Archives; and the many small town museums around the country and the many historians and genealogists who provided local knowledge. Thanks also to all those individuals and families who shared their personal recollections, and provided first-hand information about the lives of their ancestors.

Roberto Buzzolan provided the great photo for the cover, and Denene Marten photographed the gravestones and locations for Greenstone Pictures.

The television series *Epitaph* was produced with the help of New Zealand on Air and Television New Zealand.

Introduction

MAKING THE TELEVISION series *Epitaph* took me on a fantastic journey not only from one end of New Zealand to the other, but also back in time from the present to the early days of colonisation; and from lonely graves in remote inaccessible spots to the crowded, noisy graveyards of our large cities. Inscriptions on gravestones became windows to the past, and every time I stepped through one of these portals I began another exciting adventure.

I discovered that our history was raw and vital and full of incredible stories. Not just the well-known stories of figures we have deemed historically important, but also extraordinary stories about the lives of ordinary people. Many of these stories reveal the darker side of human nature — our past is full of murky deeds and dark tales — but equally, there are other stories that celebrate our noble qualities, self-sacrifice, heroism and bravery.

In some cases there was nothing to go on but a cryptic clue on a headstone: all the information had to be derived from other sources. In this regard, the *Epitaph* team of researchers did a wonderful job. Where information *was* available, we were often able to add to it; and for some stories our research folders now contain the most comprehensive collection of information that exists so far.

In New Zealand there has always been a strong tradition of storytelling, spinning ripping yarns, tall tales and true. *Epitaph* continues that tradition and proves that "Truth is stranger than fiction".

For me, as the storyteller-cum-detective investigator, bringing these stories to life has been one of the most rewarding experiences of my career. People around the country have let me into their hearts and lives, sharing intimate details of their family history. For some, I was able to return the favour by providing information about an ancestor or event of which they were unaware.

Some stories remain unresolved — a mystery. There were brick walls I could not get beyond. However, as more and more people become aware of these stories, it's possible that new information may come to light. An old letter, perhaps — something that shows the truth of Matthew 10:26: "There is nothing covered that shall not be revealed".

Auckland 1997

There is nothing covered that shall not be revealed

SACRED TO THE MEMORY OF
Bro. HUGH A. HAMILTON. G.T.
WHO MET HIS DEATH IN AN UNACCOUNTABLE MANNER
ON NOVEMBER 28TH 1882
AGED 31 YEARS
TO WHOSE MEMORY THIS STONE IS ERECTED
BY THE BRETHREN OF THE
ORANGE INSTITUTION

THERE IS NOTHING COVERED THAT SHALL NOT BE REVEALED
Matthew X XXVI

As I STOOD in Auckland's Grafton cemetery and lifted my eyes from Hugh's headstone to ponder the significance of his intriguing epitaph, they fell upon a bouquet of flowers a stone's throw away that marked the spot where a young K. Road prostitute was recently murdered. It reminded me that her murder still remained unsolved.

Was Hugh Hamilton's death 115 years ago another unsolved murder? What did it mean "unaccountable manner"? What was the "Orange Institution"? And what was the meaning of the quotation from the Bible? The roar of traffic from the nearby intersection of K. Road and Symonds Street cut short my reflections, and as I headed for the library I was left with a strong feeling that, for many reasons, Hugh Hamilton was not resting in peace.

The newspaper archives at Auckland Central City Library are always a good place to start looking for information. I thought I'd start with the *New Zealand Herald* of 29 November 1882, the day after Hugh died. Sure enough, there amongst the reports of a fatal drowning, an attempted suicide, British policy in Egypt and the advertisements for Dr Bright's Phosphodyne was the headline "SINGULAR FATAL ACCIDENT" with an account of Hugh's death. In the following day's paper, I found a full report of the coroner's inquest.

The salient facts arising out of the inquest were as follows. Mrs Hamilton, wife of the deceased, testified that on the night of Monday 27 November, Hugh left home at 10 minutes to seven to attend a meeting of the Orange Lodge at Newton Hall. She did not see him again until between one and two in the morning when he came home. Mrs Hamilton testified that Hugh had been addicted to drink for the past two years and she believed he was not sober when he came home that night. She was in bed and had a kerosene lamp burning in her room on account of her two-month-old baby being ill.

Hugh was in the habit of taking the lamp when he came in late — he and his wife Marion were at this time sleeping in different rooms. However, he did not come into the room this night because his wife had asked him not to remove the lamp as both she and the baby were unwell.

Directly after hearing him enter, Mrs Hamilton said that she heard a noise of a heavy fall, which caused a vibration through the house. She got up immediately and went to Hugh's room and found him lying on the floor, making efforts to stand. He did so, but immediately fell again. Mrs Hamilton went to the bedroom for the light, and by this time Hugh had managed to get up the second time and was groping his way towards her. She put the light down and tried to steady him, and it was then he spoke for the first time: "I have cut my head on the edge of the bed, and the blood is flowing so fast that I feel quite weak. If you would, please take me to another room. I am bound to let my missus know tonight." This is certainly an odd comment to make, not the sort of thing you would expect his wife to have made up — unless she were particularly clever. She helped him back from the passage into his room and laid him on the bed. He never spoke again and was unconscious from that time until the time of his death between 9 and 10 the next morning.

Mrs Hamilton bathed her husband's head with a sponge; he was bleeding from a large wound on the right temple. She continued to bathe the wound until 4 or 5 am.

She had nobody in the house with her but their children, so she then went next door to wake her mother and sister as she was getting alarmed. Dr Walker was sent for, and he arrived between six and seven. At this point, Mrs Hamilton became unconscious for an hour or so and her sister-in-law attended the doctor.

Dr Walker next gave evidence. He gave technical descriptions of the two wounds: a triangular wound on the right temple near the frontal bone where the skull was fractured; and an incised wound an inch long at the back of the head. He concluded a fall against the bed would be sufficient to cause the fracture but he could not account for the wound at the back of the head. There was a great deal of blood about the room and bed and also along the passage leading to Mrs Hamilton's room.

Dr Dawson, who was called in for a second opinion at about eight am, agreed death was caused by a fracture of the skull and injury to the brain by a fall against a hard substance. There was a slight smell of drink perceptible in the breath of the deceased.

An acquaintance of the deceased testified he left the deceased at 10.30 pm at the door of the lodge room at which time he was perfectly sober.

Mr Davidson, proprietor of the York Hotel, testified the deceased came into the hotel at 11.30. He was sober. He stayed for about seven minutes but had no drink.

Having listened to all the evidence, the jury returned a verdict of "accidental death".

I checked the newspaper for two or three days following, but there were no more reports. That seemed to be the end of it, but it didn't add up. Why would the Orange Order make such strong statements on Hugh's gravestone? "There is nothing covered that shall not be revealed" kept going through my mind. What was it exactly that was "covered" that needed to be "revealed"? A good mystery solver should not overlook the obvious, so I went to the Orange Order to ask them.

As the big heavy door of the Newton Orange Society clanged shut behind me, I realised I had been here before. In the late 1960s I knew it as the Orange Ballroom and came here with my mates to meet girls and dance to the beat of Herma Keil and the Keil Isles. I thought then it was called the Orange Hall because it had been painted orange.

Mrs McCready, the acting secretary, escorted me upstairs to the hallowed inner sanctum, a room that smelt of tradition, rituals and secret signs. A room in which Hugh would have spent many, probably too many, hours attending to lodge business, for I discovered he was a Grand Tyler, a sort of keeper of the door, hence the G.T. on his gravestone. He had also been secretary for three successive years, which was an indication of the high esteem with which he was regarded by his fellow Orangemen. One wall of the room we stood in was adorned with several pictures of Orange marches, one up Queen Street that Hugh could well have organised. Another wall had a large portrait of a very young Queen Elizabeth and Prince Philip, while another wall carried a huge, magnificent cloth painting of William (III) of Orange looking heroic at the Battle of the Boyne. I now realised that this was the same Orange Order that was involved in all the sectarian violence in Northern Ireland; however, Mrs McCready assured me nothing like that went on here these days. In fact, the order was in danger of dying out.

Apparently, the first lodge in New Zealand was established in Auckland in 1858, and gradually spread throughout the country so that by the time of Hugh's death there were over 40 in the North Island alone. Ostensibly, the members came from Protestant Irish backgrounds and opposed any hint of papal authority over the government in New Zealand. They strongly opposed self-government for Ireland and were often openly anti-Catholic. There were similar Catholic organisations, such as the Hibernians, and over the years a number of clashes between the two sides occurred, including two just three years before Hugh's death (one in Timaru and one in Christchurch). The Auckland Orangemen, and Hugh was probably among them, were to provoke further unrest in 1880 when they invited Canadian Pastor Charles Chiniquy, a rabidly anti-Catholic former priest, to visit the country to speak. The movement wasn't solely political, though, for its members also believed in strict adherence to the Bible and would have pursued many good deeds.

Mrs McCready had not known of Hugh Hamilton's gravestone when I telephoned her a few days earlier but, since checking the records (most of which had been destroyed), she had found a couple of significant entries in the society's minutes. One approved the cost and design of Hugh's headstone and another much more dramatic entry described Hugh's character as worthy of imitation, "a kindly and genial temperament". Mrs McCready added that as a highly esteemed Orangeman he would definitely have been teetotal as well. The minutes continue:

> . . . but it is not so much with his character that we have to deal tonight but more with the fact that an opinion exists in the minds of many that he was cruelly murdered in cold blood.

Hugh Hamilton's mother and father, Elizabeth and John Hamilton. John was a gardener and nurseryman with a business in Khyber Pass Road. Elizabeth opposed Hugh's marriage to Marion and tried to get him to break off the engagement. After Hugh's death she asked Marion, "Why did you not call in assistance?" Marion replied, "What could I do? I had a sick baby." To which Elizabeth responded, "I would have put down my baby on the bed and gone to my neighbour's house in my nightdress and stockings before I would have let a husband of mine bleed to death." COURTESY C. HAMILTON

Murder! I knew it. I knew there was a dramatic story behind this headstone. The meeting minutes went on to discuss hiring a lawyer to help the Crown prosecutor, which made me suspect a trial, and a trial meant more newspaper reports. So back to the archives I went.

If only I had scrolled on through just a few more days when I first checked for a report of Hugh's death, I would have been rewarded with the headline:

THE DEATH OF HUGH AITKEN HAMILTON
A POLICE INVESTIGATION COMMENCED

Poring over the reports that daily filled up many columns, the whole grisly episode began to reveal itself to me.

The police had been forced to act because scarcely had Hugh been buried before "Dame Rumour with her hundred tongues became busy with the case." It was well known by relatives and friends that Hugh's relatives with his wife had been of an unhappy nature for some time and that Hugh was jealous of his wife because of a Mr Priestley being a "friend of the family". Friend of the family indeed, I thought. The fact that Mrs Hamilton had sat with her wounded husband all through the hours of the early morning without calling in her own relations to help wasn't looked on too favourably either. Nor was the fact that she had undressed Hugh and put all his clothes and the sheets off the bed in a tub to be soaked; she later burnt them, along with the carpet. She had also washed and cleaned the floor. Another puzzling feature was how Hugh had managed to put away his lodgebook and regalia case neatly in their normal place, as well as wind up his watch, when he was supposedly stumbling around worse the wear for drink. Several jurymen openly expressed their dissatisfaction with the verdict, though compelled to give it on the basis of the evidence provided.

After two weeks investigating the matter, the police arrested Hugh's wife, Marion, and a young theological student with the name of *Thomas Foley Collen Priestley*.

As I sifted my way through the mass of detail that came out of the police investigations, and later the trial, I realised that I need look no further for the main players in what was proving to be a domestic tragedy — yet another version of the eternal triangle.

Hugh Aitken Hamilton was 31 at the time of his death and a native of Glasgow, a city with many ties to Ireland. He was a powerful man, about 5 feet 11 inches tall and weighing 12 stone. He worked as a storeman earning 2 pounds 10 shillings a week. He was an enthusiastic Orangeman and a regular member of the congregation at St James's Church. He was much esteemed by his relatives and friends and considered an affectionate father.

Marion was 30. She met her husband at the Fraternal Home Lodge of Good Templars, of which they were both members. The Good Templars were against the consumption of alcohol, so it is likely she would have been in sympathy with the Orange Order, though this would explain her alienation from her husband if he had taken to drink as she claimed. She had three children: Richard, the eldest, between three and four; Alexander, about two; and the baby, only a few months old. Marion took to fainting fits, believed by her unsympathetic nurse to be caused by "nervousness and temper". She was described as suffering from palpitations of the heart and having "a spare figure and unemotional looking features". Her recovery from giving birth was said at the trial to be "more tedious" than for most women, though after bearing three children in quick succession, with little medical care, it is not surprising she was ill. Both maternal and infant mortality were high at the time, with puerperal sepsis in mothers and respiratory diseases, diarrhoea and prematurity in babies being common causes of death.

Aged 19, Priestley boarded next door to Marion and Hugh Hamilton. He was a frequent visitor to the Hamilton household, especially when Hugh was not there, it would seem. He came from Hobart as a child with his mother and stepfather. The stepfather left and his mother died in 1879. He was then only 16. He had been brought up a Roman Catholic but was converted to Protestantism, and at the time of Hugh's death was undergoing instruction and education with a view to eventually becoming a minister of the Presbyterian Church. He was described as having a very religious nature.

Hugh and Marion's domestic situation was, to put it mildly, not good. Marion had many times openly expressed her feelings to others. She had said that nothing would bring her happiness but death or divorce. On another occasion she had said if it were not for her mother's grey hairs she had an offer of 50 pounds and would clear out where she would never be heard of.

The newspapers reported that Hugh was known to "chafe at the state of things in his home but seemed to lack the firmness of will to decisively put a stop to it". Marion's nurse reported an incident one Saturday night when she was called out to find Priestley in the kitchen and Hamilton running about looking for the brandy bottle. Hamilton said his wife had fainted, and in reply to a question said he would not cause his wife to faint if he was not told by people in the street about Priestley and Mrs Hamilton.

Priestley had once told a neighbour that Hamilton had quarrelled with Marion and threatened to pull her hair. Priestley said he took up a chair and told Hamilton if he touched one hair on her head he would knock him down. Hamilton replied, "It was too bad of you to interfere, Mr Priestley." Priestley had continued to the neighbour that he "would have done it and stamped the life out of him, too".

During the police investigation, neighbours had had a field day reporting Thomas and Marion's activities. They were obviously the scandal of the neighbourhood and had been indiscreet, to say the least. To quote from the newspaper of the day:

> Priestley occupied a position in the Hamilton home which no man, however platonic might be his friendship, or however exalted may be his character, or ecclesiastical his position, should occupy.

Wonderful understatement, I thought, for a man who was scarcely out of the Hamilton house, who took the children out, made them toys, and during Marion's confinement sat with her and read and prayed with her. Just whose baby was this? I wondered. Priestley was often in Marion's bedroom, he had been seen brushing her hair, bathing her face with lavender water and often brought her delicacies.

Despite his jealousy and knowledge of what was going on, Hugh, it seemed, was still in love with Marion. Even as late as the Sunday before his death, he had gathered a huge bunch of flowers from his father's residence at the Domain to give to Marion. However, I doubt this expression of love was accepted in the way Hugh would have liked, for he had replied to an enquiry about his wife that, "She is not very well in health, but worse in temper."

Much of my sympathy lay with Hugh, but as I pieced more and more of the puzzle together, my sympathy for the other two, especially Marion, began to take over. I started to imagine a possible scenario.

Marion, obviously highly strung and quite likely suffering from what we would nowadays describe as post-natal depression, was not coping. Hugh was at work during the day and being virtually married to the Orange Lodge was at meetings on many evenings. When he was home, there would be tension in the air. The marriage was on the rocks. They had not shared the same bed for at least three months. While full of good intentions, I doubt Hugh was capable of the kind of support Marion needed. Enter a young, sensitive man, who initially acts as a friend of the family but who more and more becomes involved with Marion. He spends all his time doing things for her. He's romantic. He reads poetry to her and even, as it transpired in the trial, writes poetry for her:

When wind and storm are past and gone,
Shall gentle calms succeed —
I know to ease the troubled mind,
Sleep is the rest it needs.
With these few lines I tell my mind,
You may in them a Question find.
My meaning's plain, to find it out —
Love is a torment when in doubt.

Marion Hamilton
COURTESY L. WALKER

As the prosecution took great delight in pointing out, the first word of each line read in order left no doubt as to the nature of Thomas and Marion's relationship. For Priestley, who had had such an insecure upbringing — with his mother dying three years earlier when he was 16 and no father — and for Marion with all her own needs, it was probably inevitable that they would form such a close bond. For Hugh, it meant being pushed aside in his own house. Not only was this young interloper stealing his wife's affections, but he was an ex-Catholic to boot. It meant jealousy and resentment. All round, passion was running high and I suspect things were reaching breaking point. Thomas and Marion certainly had a *motive*. So what happened on that fateful night?

The weight of circumstantial evidence against Thomas and Marion was impressive. There was the state of the marriage and the relationship with Priestley. There was Marion's strange behaviour on the night of Hugh's "accident" in not calling for a doctor till six am and bathing the wound continuously instead of trying to staunch the flow of blood with a bandage. There was the issue of drink. Marion insisted Hugh was drunk that night and that he had had a problem with drink for some time; yet there was absolutely no evidence of this. There was the strange inconsistency about the time Hugh was supposed to have come home. Witnesses last saw him leaving for home at 11.30;

yet Marion said he didn't get back until 1.30 am. Marion was seen taking an axe out into the backyard the day after Hugh died and concealing it in the long grass. The walls of Hugh's room were splashed with blood on three sides, on one wall to a height of 6 feet; yet there was no blood on the projection of the bedpost against which Hugh was supposed to have hit his head. Also this projection did not match the size of the wound. The back of the axe, however, did. It fitted the wound almost perfectly. During the trial, three doctors said it would be highly improbable if not impossible for a man to walk and

talk after such a wound. All three were also of the opinion that such a wound could not be caused by a fall against a bedstead.

When questioned about his whereabouts on the night of the murder, Priestley was unable to give a satisfactory answer. He gave three different accounts, all of which proved to be false. He even asked a friend to lie for him, but the friend refused to do this and reported this incident to the police.

It was discovered that Priestley had bought strychnine under a very dubious pretence, supposedly for a friend who wanted to get rid of some dogs. Or was it so that Hugh could meet his end in an even more painful manner?

There was a further incriminating factor. On the night Hugh died, all the children were sleeping in Marion's room in her bed; and yet the normal arrangement was for one child to sleep in a cot in the father's room and another in the bed with the father, while the baby slept with the mother.

Taken all together, things did not look good for Thomas and Marion. What astounded me was how the jury at the inquest could have returned a verdict of accidental death. This became clear to me when I came across a letter to the editor by the jury foreman John Wilkes:

Sir,

. . . The jury were hastily summoned on the morning of this terrible affair, and the evidence brought before them very brief, so much so that the general public are likely to imbibe the impression that the jury empanelled were incompetent to deal with the case. I can assert without fear of contradiction that the jury was composed of persons of intelligence and sound judgement . . . Commiseration for the widow's bereavement alone prevented the foreman asking questions, and the jury, although not altogether satisfied, could not do otherwise than they did with the evidence before them. It was the reticence of the medical gentlemen, and the demand upon their valuable time, that had something to do with a fuller inquiry into the verdict. The constable scarcely deemed it necessary to call more witnesses, indeed this functionary could do no more than he did considering the brief time allowed him to "get up" the evidence and summon the inquest . . . With regard to the production of further witnesses, the coroner seemed satisfied with the testimony of Mrs Hamilton, and her testimony of her husband being in a "state of beer", and he read the verdict over twice — accidents were accidents — and accidents were of common occurrence. I myself suggested an adjournment. The evidence before the jury was such that no other verdict could be arrived at other than "accidental death".

Evidently, the inquest jury was presented with the sight of Marion giving her testimony head down, tears flowing down her cheeks and seeming to be in such grief that Dr Philson the coroner "did not care to harrow her feelings by too minute a questioning about her husband". The jury was also aware that Marion's infant was "breathing its last".

I could now understand the accidental death verdict at the inquest, but what really surprised me, having waded through all the damning evidence produced at the trial, was that the trial jury found Marion and Thomas not guilty. It seemed incredible. Had they got away with it or were they genuinely innocent? I knew what I thought: guilty as sin. Who else killed Hugh? I now knew the significance of Hugh Hamilton's epitaph and I also knew why the Orange Order had felt that justice had not been done. As to whether the truth would one day be revealed — that I was not so sure about.

The judge in his summing up steered the jury towards not guilty. He said, "What has been set before us is a vast number of facts not linked together in the way that is necessary to constitute a chain of circumstantial evidence. They are a large number of facts calculated to raise suspicion but not to make conclusive evidence of guilt." With regard to Priestley, he said, "Are you satisfied he was there that night? Is there any evidence? Is there not an absolute want of a link to connect him with the crime, namely the proof that he was there . . . But if he is guilty she is guilty." The jury couldn't convict one without the other and they chose to convict neither.

When the jury returned its verdict to a courtroom packed with unprecedented numbers of women, many carrying babies, there was "a sensation in the court", and the few who attempted to applaud were not joined with a response from the crowd.

The judge, before discharging Priestley, said, "I will just say one word, namely that you have brought yourself into your present position by your own fault, by your indiscreet familiarity with a married woman and in endeavouring to account for your absence from your lodgings on the night in question by a falsehood. You are discharged."

To Marion he said, "You a married woman have brought yourself to this position by your indiscreet familiarity with a single man and by talking indiscriminately about your family troubles. Your case should be a warning to others not to commit such indiscretions. You are discharged."

And so, with nothing more than a severe ticking off, Thomas and Marion both walked free.

I felt sure this was a case where modern forensic techniques would have left no doubt. Out of interest, I supplied all the details of the head wounds to a modern-day criminal pathologist. He came to these conclusions: Hugh was hit in the right temple from behind by a right-handed person wielding a weapon such as an axe. From such a blow there is no way Hugh could have got to his feet again let alone spoken.

After the trial, Thomas and Marion did not stay in East Street, Newton amongst Marion's relations. I traced them to Australia, where Priestley had changed his name to Cullane and where I got the feeling they had been virtually banished. I was astonished

Marion and Thomas's marriage certificate, signed 23 years after Hugh's death

to find a marriage certificate for Thomas and Marion registered in the year 1905. Twenty-three years after Hugh's death, when Thomas was 42 and Marion 53, they married in a little town ironically called Orange. Was this a cruel joke or just one of those extraordinary coincidences? Certainly, I was pleased that they had stayed together. It indicated Thomas and Marion may have found a real and genuine love that Marion and Hugh seemed to lack. At any rate, I presume Marion must have got over her difficulties recovering from childbirth because she went on to have three more children to Thomas.

An intriguing epitaph had taken me on an interesting journey, and oddly out of all the information that I had collected it was an entry in the *Police Gazette* about three months before Hugh's death that captured my imagination more than anything else:

> Stolen on the twenty second ultimo at East St. Newton, Auckland, a green birdcage with square bottom, one leg off, containing a pure yellow canary, a good singer, property of Hugh Aitken Hamilton, value three pound ten. Identifiable.

There was something about that entry that made me feel very sad. I couldn't help but imagine Hugh finding a small amount of solace in his pet canary that he wasn't finding in Marion's arms, and I couldn't help but speculate that Marion in a fit of pique had wrung its neck!

Paying a final visit to Hugh's grave made me feel very sad over this whole affair. Why had it ended in death? Was it so difficult for Marion to leave? Couldn't she and Thomas have just run off together? As things turned out, I imagined the grey hairs Marion was

10

so anxious to avoid giving her mother must have been completely white by the end of this whole episode. I also wondered if I was wrong to feel so strongly about their guilt; after all, the judge was right, there was an element of doubt.

Hugh's grave had an indented square where it looked like a photo had once been. I had brought another to place there — a fine picture of Hugh cutting a dashing figure in all his Orangeman regalia. I slotted it in place. Standing up, my eyes once more took in the spot where the prostitute had been murdered. Fresh flowers lay there. Someone cared. And, for Hugh, I hoped he might rest easier knowing that his story had at least been told, even if that which had been covered had not been fully revealed.

Hugh Hamilton in his Orangeman regalia in happier times.
COURTESY C. HAMILTON

S *tiletto*

WELLINGTON'S OLD BOLTON STREET cemetery, like Auckland's Grafton cemetery, is not a quiet place. The motorway, which carries Wellingtonians to and from the city centre each day, has been built right through the middle of it. But in spite of the steady drone of cars passing in top gear just a few metres away, it's pleasant to walk under the large shady trees that have been left and between the haphazard lines of the old gravestones, often nearly hidden in the undergrowth.

I found the one I was looking for right beside a path in clear view. It's a small headstone with a terse inscription, which still manages to convey the shock, anger and grief felt by the family of Thomas Hawkings after his violent death over 100 years ago.

SACRED TO THE MEMORY OF
THOMAS HAWKINGS
BORN APRIL 15, 1839
MURDERED MAY 3, 1889

It's an inscription that means a great deal, yet says little. This 50-year-old man died at the hands of another, and not by accident. Who killed him, and why? Was the murderer found and punished? What did the murder mean to 1889 New Zealand, a society still alien to itself with most of its members born overseas?

Just a short walk down the road, in the massive, modern and efficient National Library building, is Alexander Turnbull's peerless collection, I found references to individual New Zealanders, compiled on an old-fashioned index card system. "Hawkings, Thomas" had several entries; the most promising seemed to be *Murder Will Out — The Mystery of Kaiwarra* by J. Evison, published in 1889 (the same year as the murder).

This little book, about 50 pages long, gave the full story of the murder and subsequent trial in colourful detail. It also contained a number of line drawings showing all the main characters in this extraordinary drama, along with the murder weapon and the murdered man's clothes, vividly overprinted with bright-red bloodstains. Clearly, this was a case that had aroused enormous interest when it took place.

As I read this convoluted nineteenth-century account of the strange and deeply tragic story of Hawkings' death, I started to picture the man and the circumstances of his murder. The crime had taken place just a few miles north of where I was sitting, in a part of Wellington that I knew. Evidently, it had conjured up passions and prejudices that are still alive and well in present-day New Zealand.

Kaiwharawhara as it was in Hawkings' day.
ALEXANDER TURNBULL LIBRARY (TOP) F10410 1/2; (BOTTOM) F51963 1/2

"Kaiwarra" is how Evison's book refers to the suburb of Kaiwharawhara, a steep-sided gorge just two miles outside Wellington City that runs back from the harbour towards Porirua and the main highway north. Thomas Hawkings was a prosperous farmer who had owned a large, hilly property on the north side of the gorge. Today it is densely packed with expensive homes and 180° views of Wellington Harbour. In 1889, he and his wife Mary had been there for 18 years, and nine children and several farm workers lived with them in a handsome two-storey house, high on a ridge in an area now called Khandallah.

Every Friday, Hawkings took his horse and trap into town to sell his produce and bank the cash. On 31 May 1889, he set off as usual in the morning but by 6 pm, dinnertime, he had not returned. A few hours later, his wife's cousin, who was staying with the family, set out with a lantern and found Hawkings' body lying face-down in the road. A post-mortem

next day found 21 stab wounds and two gunshot wounds in the neck, chest and back.

Police detectives searched the road where the body was found and discovered some bloodstained stones, scattered newspaper and a broken knife. They spoke to Mrs Hawkings and she told them her late husband didn't like being on the road after dark because he was afraid of one of his tenants, Louis Chemis. Chemis was a road-mender who lived nearby and leased some of Hawkings' land. The two men had recently had a dispute over the lease, and Mrs Hawkings said Chemis had sworn at and threatened her husband.

Louis Chemis was then aged 34, an Italian who had arrived in Wellington as a sailor 12 years before. He worked as a labourer for the Hutt City Council, and he and his Irish wife Annie milked a few cows on the land they leased from Hawkings and delivered the fresh milk on foot each morning. They were at home with their five small children on the night after the murder, when two police officers arrived with a search warrant. They found a double-barrelled shotgun, some pieces of newspaper and a rusty stiletto (a small knife with a narrow, double-edged blade).

Four days later, after an inquest showed that a stiletto-type knife had been used to kill Hawkings, Chemis was arrested. He did not resist the police and told his family, "I won't be there long."

Chemis was very wrong about this. He was refused bail and kept in jail for more than a week until his appearance at

Thomas Hawkings (above) with his jacket (below), showing how frenzied his attacker had been. ABOVE: COURTESY T.G. HAWKINGS; BELOW: FROM J. EVISON, *MURDER WILL OUT*

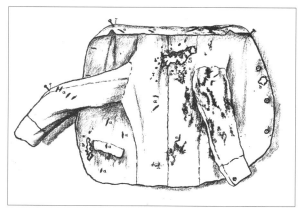

a packed Wellington Magistrates' Court. The evidence against him hinged on a piece of newpaper found at his home that police said matched a piece used to make a wad for the shotgun cartridge fired at Hawkings. Chemis was sent back to jail until the next sitting of the Supreme Court.

On 8 July, the Supreme Court was filled to overflowing as the prosecutor told the jury that such a horrible crime could never have been committed by an Englishman. Chemis was defended by a young lawyer named Charles Bunny, who tried to prove that Hawkings had many arguments with his neighbours and family, as well as with his client. By the fifth day of the trial, Bunny was obviously unwell and feeling the strain. When the prosecution had completed its case, he announced, to the astonishment of the whole court, that he did not intend to call any defence witnesses. These witnesses were already waiting in another room to give their evidence and had to be sent home. It now seems that Bunny made his extraordinary decision simply because he felt so ill he wanted the trial to finish as quickly as possible.

Louis Chemis's house.
FROM J. EVISON, *MURDER WILL OUT*

The following day, Bunny attacked the crucial prosecution evidence regarding the piece of newspaper supposedly found at Chemis's house. This fragment, he said, could easily have been mixed up by the police with another piece found at the scene of the crime. He pointed out that poachers were often seen on Hawkings' land, and the dead farmer had had a lot of trouble with them. He warned the jury about convicting on the basis of circumstantial evidence, then sank exhausted into his chair.

In his summing up, the judge said, "it is evident that the murder was committed with a weapon which is in common use amongst the nation to which this prisoner belongs . . . ". After several hours, the jury returned and the foreman pronounced Chemis "guilty".

At this, Annie Chemis, who had sat in the courtroom throughout the trial, collapsed in loud sobbing and was led outside. Louis himself did not seem to understand that the trial was over. He told the judge once again that he was innocent, and insisted he could prove it with the help of witnesses. But the judge, wearing his black cap over his wig, replied that the prosecution case had been fair, and the defence case "able". He sentenced Louis Chemis to death by hanging.

Louis's lawyer, Charles Bunny, was not in court to hear this sentence pronounced. He was by then desperately ill in bed with typhoid fever. Two days after his client's death sentence, he died.

All over the country, people were talking about the Hawkings murder case. The main newspapers expressed astonishment that Chemis had been convicted on such flimsy evidence. A petition to the

Louis Chemis
COURTESY P. CHEMIS

15

Governor of New Zealand was started, calling for Chemis's death sentence to be commuted to life imprisonment. The petition also claimed that an innocent man had been wrongly convicted, saying:

> Time will unfold the mystery, remove the doubt surrounding it, and reveal the true murderer, whomsoever it may be.

In the next few days, nearly 9000 people signed the petition, and they included several members of the jury who had just convicted Louis.

Two weeks after the sentencing, the petition was presented to the Governor, Lord Onslow. He took careful note of its arguments, met with Louis Chemis's wife Annie, her daughter Lizzie, and Thomas Hawkings' widow Mary, and announced that Louis Chemis's death sentence was commuted to "penal servitude for life".

This was not nearly good enough for the persistent Annie Chemis, who was determined to prove her husband's innocence. One of the most contentious elements of the Crown case was the evidence and conduct of the police officers who had first searched the Chemis house. In court, the three officers had denied finding dead quail and other items, which indicated that Louis had recently used his shotgun for hunting. This evidence totally conflicted with Louis', and suggested a possible police cover-up.

Soon after the trial ended, the Commissioner of Police himself wrote to the Minister of Justice, regretting that some members of his force had shown "almost criminal negligence . . . in their preliminary investigation" into the murder.

Annie engaged the most notorious lawyer of the day, Edwin Jellicoe — a man noted for his lack of respect for the legal establishment — to bring a charge of perjury against two of the police officers. The perjury trial began in late August and featured angry exchanges between Jellicoe, the judge, and the lawyers defending the police. Jellicoe accused the police of, among other things, planting crucial evidence (torn pieces of the *Evening Post* newspaper, said to have been used as a wad for the shotgun cartridge that killed Hawkings). The perjury case was finally thrown out by the Supreme Court, but not before further doubt was thrown on the methods used to convict Louis Chemis.

The fragments of newspaper used as evidence — were they planted on Chemis?

And that is where *Murder Will Out* ended — with Chemis in jail for life, his wife and lawyer still fighting to free him, and the whole country, including leading politicians, arguing about his trial. The final paragraph of the book reads:

"Murder will out" has passed into a proverb; all true men will join with us in the earnest hope that the truth of that proverb may be demonstrated in this case, and that Louis Chemis, if innocent, may be returned to his home and guiltless little children; or, if guilty, that his guilt may be made apparent, and the police and other innocent persons at present, in the estimation of some, resting under a stigma, may be relieved from all imputations.

By the time I finished reading this powerful little book, I had real sympathy for the surviving Hawkings family, but also for Louis Chemis. Here was an immigrant who spoke English only with difficulty, whose family clearly loved and supported him, who appeared quite innocent of this shocking crime. He seemed to have been jailed mainly through suspicion of his nationality, which may have led the police to fake part of the case against him.

I was determined to find out what happened to Louis. Did he serve out his sentence, or was Annie's struggle to free him successful? Was his innocence finally proved and, if so, was the real murderer ever found?

I was also keen to learn what had become of the families of both Louis Chemis and Thomas Hawkings. They each had several children, and perhaps their descendants still lived in the same area. Fortunately for me, both men had unusual surnames. The Wellington phonebook revealed one entry for Chemis and several for Hawkings. Soon I was speaking with Peter Chemis, great-grandson of Louis, who knew plenty about his great-grandfather's case and was quite willing to talk with me about it. We arranged to meet at his house one evening after work.

The current Chemis family — Peter, his wife Jane, and their baby son — live in Brooklyn, high above Wellington City with a panoramic view across the city lights and the harbour beyond. Both Peter and Jane are lawyers, and this gives them special interest in a case that has entered New Zealand legal history. It's hard to escape the irony of Peter Chemis and his wife ending up as part of the system that appears to have failed Peter's great-grandfather so badly.

It is important to Peter to clear the shame and disgrace that has attached to his family since the trial. Growing up in Wellington as a boy, he heard very little about his great-grandfather or the sensational events that surrounded him. Most early family photos and other records were destroyed after Louis' death, and Peter's older relatives were unwilling to talk about their ancestor who had arrived here from Italy with such disastrous consequences.

Peter's legal training helped convince him of Louis' innocence. He and Jane have called their son Louis, and they want him to grow up

The current Chemis family

Louis' young family. COURTESY P. CHEMIS

to be proud of his name and of his Italian blood. They lent me several photos of Louis, Annie and their five children, to help with my research. They also confirmed what I had begun to learn from other reading about this case — Louis' fate after he was sent to prison.

Although Annie Chemis and her lawyer kept up pressure on the courts and authorities, and they were joined by other high-powered supporters, including the Picton MP Charles Houghton Mills, their efforts to win Louis' release from prison did not persuade the government. After some time at Auckland's Mt Eden Prison, he was transferred to Lyttelton Gaol near Christchurch. There he became so depressed that he attempted suicide by cutting his arm with a sharp piece of tin. The Catholic chaplain of the jail wrote to Premier Atkinson (the equivalent of the prime minister) to urge for his release. He added *"Dubium, favet reo"* ("When in doubt, judge favourably").

Annie Chemis, who fought for her husband's innocence to be acknowledged.
COURTESY P. CHEMIS

It became plain that the government's refusal to respond to these requests was motivated more by politics than justice. If the police were shown to have acted improperly in getting a conviction, then the implications for the law of the land were serious. Even though a growing number of parliament-arians had come to believe in Louis' innocence, the Cabinet could not agree with them without admitting the police had been wrong about his case in the beginning.

Finally, after Louis had spent eight years in jail, a political solution presented itself. The year 1897 marked Queen Victoria's record-breaking 60 years as monarch of the British Empire, including New Zealand. The government decided, as part of the celebrations, to grant an amnesty to several prisoners. This would not be a declaration of their innocence, but simply a show of mercy. Louis Chemis was released from Lyttelton Jail on 22 June 1897. The day before, Annie Chemis travelled down from Wellington so she could be at the prison gate to greet him.

One might think that for the Chemis family the nightmare was over. Unfortunately, this was not the case. By the time Louis returned home to his family, they had left their small house in Kaiwarra and were living in Thorndon. Every morning, Annie got up at 3 am and went to work as a cleaner at Parliament Buildings, a job often given to the wives of men imprisoned for long periods of time, and one that Annie held for more than 30 years. But Louis was a well-known ex-convict, and he found it much more difficult to get work. He spent some months as a bricklayer working on the extensions to Parliament House, and I had to wonder whether this was a job Louis was given to assuage the conscience of a government that had put politics before his innocence. Apart from this, he mostly walked the streets looking for work, or sat around the house during the day. Presumably, he began to feel that he was just another mouth to feed, and that his family had been better off when he was in prison.

On the night of October 1898, like Thomas Hawkings nine years earlier, Louis didn't come home to dinner. Next day, his horrified family learnt that he had bought dynamite, a detonator cap and some brandy, then walked up Mt Victoria, the hill that overlooks Wellington City. There he drank the brandy, put the dynamite and detonator in his mouth, and lit the fuse. He died instantly.

From violent beginning to tragic end, the story of Louis Chemis and Thomas Hawkings was undoubtedly a deeply dramatic one. So, I was excited but not greatly surprised when Peter told me that a play had been written about his great-grandfather's case, and performed by a local theatre company some years ago. I rang the theatre and found the actors deep in rehearsals for their next production. None of them knew of a play about an Italian charged with murder late last century. However, they offered to leave a note on the theatre wall, asking anyone who knew of this play to give me a ring.

The call came a week later. The director of *The Senegallian's Spring — The Tragedy of Louis Chemis* had seen my note during a passing visit to the theatre. Like almost everyone I met who had become aware of this story, she was eager to help me and keen to establish Louis' innocence. In her house, buried in native bush within sound of the Wellington coast, she gave me the script of the play and, even better, the unpublished manuscript of an entire book on the same subject, called *Louis Chemis — A Tragedy*. My research materials were starting to pile up.

Both the book and the play had been written by an actor and local historian named Des Swain, who had died a few years earlier. In the foreword to his bulky manuscript, he explained that his mother had grown up in the Kaiwharawhara Gorge and went to school with Chemis children. It was not until he had really begun exploring the case that Swain learnt, to his astonishment, that his own grandfather had been a member of the jury that originally convicted Chemis of murder. He wrote the book, he said, "to try to redress an ancestor's error".

Des Swain's careful compilation of the documents and events surrounding the murder, the trial and its tragic aftermath was the best possible summary I could have had. But an aspect of the story was still missing, and that was the viewpoint of the Hawkings family. Their farming ancestor had been cruelly and suddenly taken from them, and their loss seemed almost to have been forgotten amid the later controversies surrounding the case.

So I tried each of the Hawkings listed in the Wellington phonebook. They all proved to be related, although the younger members of the family knew very little about the murder. They suggested I talk to another Thomas Hawkings, the grandson of the murdered man, who lives in Levin, about 100 km north of Wellington.

Thomas junior is an alert and active pensioner, and, unlike Peter Chemis, he grew up with no sense of shame about the tragedy that befell his family before he was born. His namesake's untimely death was a regular subject of conversation at family gatherings and, understandably perhaps, the Hawkings relations still feel a strong sense of grievance over the murder and don't accept that the wrong man was convicted for it. Guilty or not, Louis' conviction would have been important for them so that the awful murder could be sealed off in their minds. They would have been ready to believe it was Chemis to put an end to the terrible event.

Thomas told me that after his grandfather's death, his wife Mary found it impossible to maintain the large farm. Before long the whole estate was swallowed up in lawyer's fees, the Hawkings family left the area, and in 1910 the homestead and farm buildings were sold for removal. It became obvious that the repercussions of this incident were far-reaching for both families. Thomas lent me photographs of his grandfather and grandmother and their old home, and added a few fascinating details to their story. His grandfather's name, he said, was really Bowden, and like Louis Chemis he was originally a seaman who jumped ship in the region of Kaiwharawhara Gorge and settled there. Throughout his life, said his grandson, the older Thomas sheltered other runaway sailors who came ashore at the tiny beach at the foot of the gorge.

This was a very different Thomas Hawkings from the man who emerged during the murder trial. Louis' lawyer pictured the murdered man as a shrewd and sometimes dishonest businessman, constantly in dispute with his neighbours and relatives. His descendants remember him as warm and generous. Clearly, reviving memories of this case would also revive some of the controversy that originally surrounded it.

Another significant element of the story I still needed to investigate was the question of racial prejudice. The prosecution case and some of the press publicity coverage of the trial tended to assume that Chemis was the likely murderer simply because he was Italian, and therefore excitable, untrustworthy and prone to wield a knife. To find out more about Italian migrants in New Zealand, I tried Wellington's wonderful Central Public Library. The only history of Italian immigration to the Wellington region I could find was a recent book, *Alla Fine del Mondo – To the Ends of the Earth*, edited by Paul Elenio, deputy editor of Wellington's *Evening Post*. (Ironically, this same newspaper played a key role in the trial of Louis Chemis; those newspaper fragments in the shotgun wound were from the *Post*.)

Paul Elenio readily agreed to meet me in his downtown office. He said his own family had arrived from Italy soon after World War II. Even in those relatively recent times, he could recall the suspicion and hostility felt by many New Zealanders towards people who ate olive oil instead of butter, and whose country had just been at war with our own. During the war many Italians were interned, some for five years, and those not locked up were regularly watched by police and were moved if they lived by the sea in case they signalled to the enemy — so despite being New Zealanders, they were treated as betrayers.

In Paul Elenio's view, when Louis Chemis lived here, public knowledge of other countries and cultures would have been even more limited. Like Louis, most Pakeha New Zealanders had been born elsewhere, but generally in solidly Anglo-Saxon Britain.

The small Italian fishing communities around the Wellington coastline were isolated from wider society by barriers of language and religion as well as location. Because of this, the general attitude towards "the Latin races" — that they were hot-tempered but cowardly and irrationally violent — remained unchallenged by everyday reality.

Louis Chemis and his defenders offered the court ample evidence that he was a reliable long-term employee, a devoted family man and a valued member of his community who had never previously offended in any way. It didn't help him. He looked and sounded different from the people around him, including every member of his jury, and the dangerous reputation given his race outweighed evidence of his own character.

In particular, Chemis was fatally implicated by the nature of Hawkings' murder. As well as two gunshots, death was caused by a horrifying frenzy of stab-wounds, apparently delivered with tremendous force by someone in a furious rage. When a traditional Italian stiletto was found in the Chemis house, and the coroner testified that it could have caused the knife-wounds, the prosecution felt their case was practically watertight. It didn't matter that the stiletto was very rusty, showed no sign of blood, and was not concealed in any way. It didn't even matter that some other observers felt the wounds weren't caused by Louis' tiny knife at all but by some other double-edged blade such as a butcher's knife. The thinking tended to run — Italians use stilettos, Chemis is an Italian, he owns a stiletto: case closed.

Why were Italians such a threat, I wondered? What did this say about these nineteenth-century settlers? Were they so unsure of themselves in their earnest endeavours to establish a solid foothold in this country that anything culturally different was a threat? But then again, when I think of the recent reactions against Asian immigration, I wonder whether we have come any further.

What had happened to this damning and notorious little knife — the stiletto? I wondered whether it still existed in police files after all these years. The place to start looking was the New Zealand Police Museum, out at the Police College in Porirua. Regretfully, curator Anna Parkin explained that the museum exhibits, including a gruesome display of homemade pistols, a hangman's rope and a homemade whisky still, only dated from about the turn of the century. She could find no records of the Chemis case on her files, but she promised to ring me if anything turned up.

To my amazement, she rang a few days later in high excitement. A retired policeman had just turned up at the museum with an armload of old logbooks and dropped them on her desk, saying she might find them interesting. Turning the thick, faded pages, each one giving the photograph and physical description of an arrested man held at Johnsonville Police Station, a familiar name jumped out at her.

A typical stiletto of the type owned by Chemis.
PHOTO: SIMON YOUNG

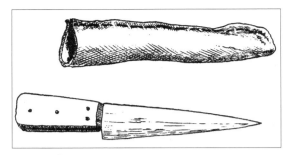

A sketch of the sheath knife found later at the scene of the crime. FROM *MURDER WILL OUT*

There was just one more piece of the puzzle I wanted to find. If Chemis didn't kill Hawkings (and I now felt certain that he didn't), who was the real murderer? During and after the trial, a variety of other possible killers had been suggested, ranging from Mary Hawkings' brother George Bowles, to a farming acquaintance named William Lidden. In 1896, when Louis had been imprisoned for seven years, a sensational announcement came from a New South Wales jail, according to Des Swain's book. Samuel Trudgeon, a New Zealander, convicted thief and jail escaper, confessed to the killing and claimed to have buried the murder weapons in Wellington's Bolton Street Cemetery — where the gravestone which began this story now stands. The cemetery was searched, and Trudgeon's story was investigated by police, but finally disregarded as publicity-seeking.

There was at least one more possible suspect, whom Des Swain considers the most likely to have committed the crime. Several witnesses at the trial gave evidence of seeing a strange man near the murder scene some weeks before Hawkings' death. He was probably a poacher after hares and quail, and Hawkings was known to be very angry about the activities of poachers on his property. A dead hare was found near his murdered body, suggesting that Hawkings arrived in his pony-trap soon after hearing a shot, argued with the poacher and was killed by him, perhaps in a drunken rage. A bloody sheath knife which could have caused the stab wounds, was found near the scene some days later. Amazingly, this was not admitted as evidence by the police, who were satisfied that they already had their man. The nameless poacher, described by some witnesses as having a large, unkempt moustache, seems to have got clean away.

More than 100 years on, it's highly unlikely that the real circumstances of the Kaiwarra murder will ever be known. All we can hope is that some lessons have been learnt from this tragic story. The more recent but similar case of Arthur Allan Thomas suggests that a little progress has been made. In 1971 Thomas was also convicted of murder amid allegations of planted police evidence. Like Chemis, he served eight years before being released, and the precedent of Louis Chemis's amnesty was referred to in the newspapers at that time. However, Thomas was paid one million dollars by the government in compensation and granted a free pardon, while Chemis didn't receive a thing, not even formal acknowledgment from the government that it had erred in imprisoning him. This may well have contributed to the depression that soon killed him.

Today, Louis' great-grandson feels it's not too late for the government to remedy the wrongs of the past. Just as Waitangi Treaty grievances are being settled retrospectively, and World War II crimes acknowledged at long last, the Chemis family is hoping that the government will finally clear Louis' name.

The final feeling I am left with is great sadness at the way Louis Chemis was treated just because of his nationality. Ironically, today we can't seem to get enough of things Italian: cafés, restaurants, designer clothes and cars, wine . . . the list goes on. Italians have made their mark on our culture and we are very much the richer for it.

 *he Waikino School Tragedy*

IN WAIHI CEMETERY, THERE is a grave whose inscription is only readable when the light is at a certain angle. It says:

CHARLES STEWART
KILLED IN THE WAIKINO SCHOOL TRAGEDY
19 OCTOBER 1923
AGED 9½ YEARS

Nearby is another grave and the inscription is still clear. It reads:

KELVIN MCLEAN
KILLED IN THE WAIKINO SCHOOL TRAGEDY
19 OCTOBER 1923
OH MEMORIES

23

I didn't know it when I first visited these graves, but in October 1923 more than a thousand people had gathered at this site for the funeral of these two young boys, "Killed in the Waikino School tragedy". What happened on this date at the Waikino School?

When I made enquiries about locating the school, I was told it was impossible. Shortly after the 19 October 1923, the school mysteriously burnt down. Thinking back to the Port Arthur massacre, I wondered if the Waikino inhabitants, like those of Port Arthur, had purged themselves of a memory too horrible to look upon?

I had no idea what this tragedy could have been. I didn't recall ever having heard about a school tragedy in New Zealand. Yet, there it was. The *New Zealand Herald* of 19 October carried the report of an incident that very morning. There were nine headlines one after the other: "APPALLING CRIME" cried the first; "MANIAC IN A SCHOOL" pronounced the second; and the third in bold type read, "WILD SHOTS WITH PISTOL".

Having seen the two graves in the cemetery, I knew that the worst had happened. What I couldn't imagine was how it all might have transpired in a small town like Waikino.

Waikino lies just out of Waihi, on the road to Paeroa at the base of the Coromandel Peninsula. The town owes its existence to the establishment of the Victoria Gold Battery in 1897. Those who weren't miners were farmers or store keepers. The school was opened in 1906. Mr Reid had been headmaster of the school since 1915 and had seen it through the difficult war years. Everyone measures hardship differently, and I couldn't help smiling to myself when I found a copy of *From Slate to Computer; 100 years of Education in the Waihi and Surrounding Districts*, in which the author complained that there were never enough funds for the annual Waikino School picnic during the war.

October 19 was a Friday. The school was just one building, not more than 20 metres square, consisting of two main rooms, with standard two to six in one room and

The Waikino Gold Battery. AUCKLAND CITY LIBRARIES A12352

standard one and the primers across the hall. Crammed into these on that Friday were 140 pupils, the headmaster Mr Reid and five teachers.

What exactly happened at 10 o'clock that morning will never be known because no two accounts of an incident are ever the same. Accounts published in the newspapers and later by the Crown prosecutor, Vincent Meredith in a book called *The Long Brief* all differ slightly. But on that Friday morning, a tragedy unfolded, something like this:

Mr Reid was inside the building and the school dog started barking, something Reid said later it had never done before. The dog was putting up a challenge to one of the local farmers, John Higgins, who was walking toward the main door of the school. In a small town where everyone knows everyone, Reid knew Higgins as an Irishman, then in his mid-50s, who had emigrated to New Zealand from Canada and who had a wife and two boys. Higgins was farming locally, but he wasn't making much of a living off his land and worked in the mines to supplement his income. What Reid didn't know, but was soon to find out, was that Higgins was armed.

As Higgins came through the front door, he said, "I am here for revenge." Reid said later that one look at Higgins was enough to convince him that something was very wrong. He bundled Higgins into his study and closed the door. Higgins immediately produced an automatic pistol and stood his ground, with it pointed at Reid's stomach. He told Reid that for the last 15 years he had been persecuted, and now he was going to shoot up some of the children, and that he wasn't afraid to meet his God. Higgins actually told the headmaster to leave the school grounds, saying to him, "You are one of the three men in this world whom I respect." But Reid would never have walked away from those children, not even if he had known what it would cost him.

Standing with an automatic Colt pistol pointed at his stomach, the headmaster continued to talk to Higgins, desperately trying to convince the man to abandon his course. He told Higgins to leave the school and go to the battery to take his grievance up with the children's parents, but Higgins was beyond reasoning. In a last attempt to shield the children, Reid boldly informed Higgins he would have to shoot him before he could shoot the children. Higgins appeared unmoved by Reid's bravado.

The two men had talked for a long time. Reid remembers this well, because Higgins looked at his watch at one point and said, "I have given you twenty-five minutes and I would have given that time to no other man in the world." After more pleading on Reid's part, Higgins finally seemed to shake himself out of the grip of Reid's words and said, "You will have it then, take it." A shot rang out. Reid collapsed and tried to shout a warning as Higgins strode out of his study toward the classrooms, but he couldn't make a sound. Higgins had shot him at close range in the throat.

The next person to see John Higgins was the infant teacher Miss Kendon. She had heard the shot in the study and was then confronted with Higgins walking straight into her classroom. He ignored her and fired two shots at the children, hitting one boy in the hand. Without pausing, Higgins turned and crossed the corridor into the infants' classroom.

Pandemonium broke out with the sounds of shooting in the infants' room, and children in the other classes were leaping out of windows, cowering under desks and being rushed outside by the teachers. Desks were overturned and scattered, books and materials littered the floor, bags and coats were flung about as the children panicked and

Waikino School. FROM SLATE TO COMPUTER, COURTESY B.J. STUBBS

ran. Higgins shot at the children scrambling to get out the windows and doors and then strode up and down the rows firing under the desks where some children were hiding. One boy who knew Higgins well was 13-year-old Kelvin McLean. Shot once but only wounded, Kelvin was heard to say to Higgins, "Don't hurt me, Mr Higgins, remember I bring you firewood." Higgins shot him again, at point blank range. Charles Stewart was also shot at close range and killed as he tried to make a run for it. Four other children were shot, and two were injured jumping from windows.

Somehow, the teachers managed to get all the children away from the school building to the bottom of the schoolyard. Once the children were finally all safe, the teachers were horrified to see one boy racing back toward the schoolhouse. They called desperately after him, but he made it back up the hill and disappeared inside the building. Then, as quickly as he had gone, he reappeared racing down the hill to rejoin his classmates, only this time he was carrying the lunch he had left behind in his desk in the chaos of escaping!

The boy was fortunate that Higgins had, by then, abandoned the classrooms and returned to the study. Here he barricaded himself in by piling a sofa and other furniture up against the door. He had a position of considerable advantage with a clear view of the school grounds toward the town.

Reid heard Higgins walk over to him and he was rolled over. Higgins muttered, "He's done for," and Reid heard him walk out again into the corridor. Moments later, he was back, all the while muttering to himself. Reid heard paper being thrown into the bottom of the library cupboard. Higgins then tried to jam Reid feet first into the cupboard. Failing in this, he grabbed Reid by the shoulder and was dragging him across the floor when suddenly great shouts were heard outside. The men from the battery had come.

The shooting had been heard in the town, and word quickly made it to the battery.

26

The men dropped everything and ran. Fathers and grandfathers of the children ran the distance between the battery and the school, but when they arrived unarmed they were confronted with Higgins at the window of the study. Higgins called out, "What do you want?" and shot at them, forcing them to take cover and keep at a distance. Some of the men left and returned with an odd assortment of weapons, including a couple of revolvers and a pea gun and a rifle, and, when Sergeant O'Grady and Constable Olsen from the Waihi Police arrived, one of the miners was exchanging fire with Higgins through the window. When O'Grady told Higgins to come out, the reply came back, "No, we will have a bit of a go first," followed by a shot from Higgins that was meant for O'Grady but missed.

One of the classrooms after Higgins had been arrested. COURTESY B. J. STUBBS.

While this was going on, two miners went into the schoolroom to retrieve the bodies of the two boys. The feeling among the men gathered was running high. They wanted to storm the place and deal with Higgins then and there. One of the miners called out to Higgins that he would burn the place down with Higgins in it, and Higgins called back, "Let her go." Reid was prone on the study floor, unable to move or speak for the duration of the stand-off between the gunman and the police, but he was slipping in and out of consciousness and remembers nothing of the showdown.

Olsen and O'Grady were determined to figure a way to get Higgins, but even from within the schoolhouse they couldn't flush him out. Shots had been fired through the study door, but Higgins protected himself from a rear attack by using the cupboard door as a shield, and one of the shots had caught Mr Reid in the leg where he was still lying, so this course was abandoned.

Finally, O'Grady took a spade to the door, wanting to get a sight line into the room so they could get a shot at Higgins. Olsen lined up to fire, but Higgins fired first, badly wounding Olsen. Sergeant O'Grady ripped the rest of the door down and told Higgins if he didn't throw his gun out of the window he would shoot him dead. Higgins complied. Higgins also had a knife, but he dropped it when ordered.

Seeing the gun come out the window, the miners knew Higgins was unarmed and rushed into the study. One of the angry men landed a boot to Higgins' face, and if the policemen hadn't been present, Higgins could well have been killed. Higgins was arrested and taken away. A later search of the study found three eight-inch plugs of gelignite to which fuses had already been fitted. If any of the bullets being fired into the study had hit the gelignite, Higgins, Reid and the two policemen would have been killed.

27

Higgins, being led away by the police. AUCKLAND
WEEKLY NEWS 1 NOV. 1923, COURTESY *NZ HERALD*

What Vincent Meredith, the Crown solicitor, remembers most clearly about Higgins' trial was the crowded women's gallery and the reaction of those women to the reading of the charges on the first day of the trial. Meredith was narrating the events of the morning of Friday 23 October 1923, and having dealt with the shooting of Reid he began to recount the shootings of Kelvin McLean and Charles Stewart. At this point, a muffled sob was heard in the gallery, which started a wave of sobbing that continued for the rest of Meredith's address to the court.

The court report in the newspapers gives the first real descriptions of John Higgins: "A big lean rawboned man with a short grizzled moustache, greying hair and the bronzed face of one who spends most of his time in the open." Higgins was quiet and composed in court, and in a number of newspapers the reporters noted that he didn't appear to appreciate the enormity of what he had done.

Higgins was indeed, according to the defence, unaware of what he was doing at the time. The plea was insanity. After the shooting, he had talked to Sergeant O'Grady about the events of the fateful morning. When O'Grady asked him why he had gone to the school, Higgins said he couldn't remember, though he did recall having an argument and shooting Mr Reid, but he couldn't remember what the argument had been about. Questioned about the dynamite, Higgins told O'Grady he'd been carrying it round for a few days but wasn't sure what his intention had been, and when the subject of the shooting in the classrooms was raised, Higgins said, "I must have been crazy."

The decision for the jury was not whether or not Higgins was guilty of murder, but whether, due to insanity, he was legally responsible for his acts. The jury took only one hour and five minutes to find Higgins guilty. He was sentenced to death, which was later commuted to life imprisonment. He was incarcerated at the Avondale Asylum, which was an indication that, although found guilty, Higgins was not in fact responsible for his actions. He died at the asylum in 1928.

THERE'S NOT MUCH LEFT of Waikino now. Certainly the place bears little resemblance to what it must have been in its heyday when hundreds of men worked at the battery. What was left of the shops was swept away in a flood a few years ago. And, of course, the school has gone. It burned down very soon after the shooting.

Jack Higgins is John Higgins' oldest son. He still lives near Waikino and remembers the day of the tragedy "too clearly". Jack was at home when the police came to the door to tell his mother what had happened. He was just short of his fifteenth birthday, and he and his father had been in Waikino that morning selling firewood. His father told him to take the team of horses home, as he had some business in town to attend to.

Jack remembers Waikino as a town of good people, "Most of them from the home country," and that all the men worked together in the battery. Their farm was a couple

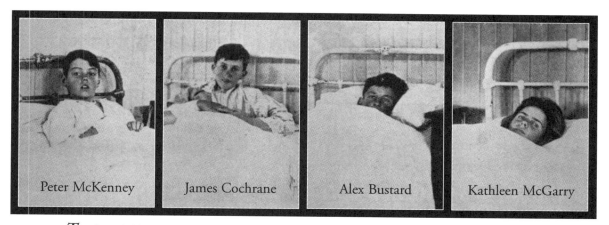

| Peter McKenney | James Cochrane | Alex Bustard | Kathleen McGarry |

The four children wounded in the shooting recuperating in the local hospital. AUCKLAND WEEKLY NEWS 1 NOV. 1923, COURTESY *NZ HERALD*

of miles out of town, but Jack knew a lot of the kids at the school, he had been a pupil there himself, but had left when he was 12 to work on the farm. He knew Mr Reid well and liked him. He remembers that Mr Reid was one of the few people his father had a good word to say about. He also remembers that one of the children shot that day was the daughter of his father's best friend. But Jack Higgins' abiding memory of the days after the awful tragedy was the visit of Mrs McLean, whose son Kelvin had been shot and killed. She had come to share her grief and sympathy with Mrs Higgins, and Jack, now in his 80s, says he can still see those two women standing in the kitchen with their arms around each other, crying.

The funeral for the dead boys. AUCKLAND WEEKLY NEWS 1 NOV. 1923, COURTESY *NZ HERALD*

Never during that terrible time, nor in all the years since, has anyone ever said a bad word to Jack about what his father did. There was no ill feeling among the locals toward the Higgins family. Waikino was a town united in shock and grief, and the Higgins family were cared for as were all those affected.

Jack didn't see his father after the shooting until he appeared in the Magistrates' Court in Paeroa. After the trial early in 1924, Jack left Waikino with his younger brother and mother to return to Canada, where they had relatives. The townspeople of Waikino helped to raise the money needed for the family to emigrate. Jack remembers being excited about the prospect of travel and it was only in hindsight that he realised what a terrible time it must have been for his mother. Their return to Canada turned out to be temporary. Three years later, they got a letter from John Higgins begging them to return to New Zealand. They came back straight away.

John Higgins was still at the Avondale Asylum and very ill. Jack was with his father when he died there in 1928. Not once did John Higgins or anyone else ever mention the tragedy at the school. Jack says it was as if it had never happened. His father talked about day-to-day concerns at the asylum, and the family talked about their work and how everybody was getting on.

When a tragedy like this strikes, the natural question is, "Why?" There is seldom an answer. Jack Higgins believes something like this had been brewing for quite a while. He describes his father as a suspicious man. He remembers he used to talk to himself a lot, but he doesn't remember him as depressed or obviously ill, although he wasn't a happy man. Jack believes this was a result of an accident his father had suffered 15 years before the shooting, while working in the mines in America. An explosion at the mine left John Higgins with head injuries. After the accident, his personality changed; he became moody and withdrawn. As he got older, his paranoia and discontent grew.

The actions of a single individual can have monstrous consequences. In the last few years many families in New Zealand have had to face the devastating aftermath of seemingly mindless killing. What amazed and inspired me when I talked to Jack Higgins were his memories of a community that had the strength to face their pain with humanity and generosity toward the family of the murderer. When we were talking, Jack said he wasn't sure people now would be as compassionate to a family in the same situation as they were to the Higgins family in Waikino in 1923. But while this small community was able to forgive, there is no question that, with the burning down of the school, they also wished to forget.

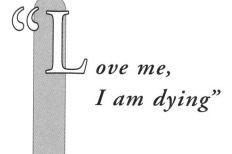

"**L**ove me,
I am dying"

SIMON YOUNG

FOR MY NEXT JOURNEY into the past, I returned to a now-familiar graveyard — Auckland's Grafton cemetery — and entered through the gate that joins the ramparts of Grafton Bridge. I was here to find Emily Keeling. A letter I had received told me she was buried somewhere on the east side of this graveyard. Just inside the Grafton Bridge entrance is the grave of Governor Hobson. His farewell is cast in bronze and set into a vast concrete slab that covers the gravesite.

Crossing under the bridge, I picked my way through the boxes, bottles and aerosol cans left by the streetkids — the remains of their last resting place. I found the slope steep and noticed the graves were further apart. This was the last section of the graveyard to be filled before it was closed in 1886. The sun rarely reaches this slope and the air is cold. Continuing down the hill alongside the bridge, I looked over the wrought-iron railing of the first grave I passed, and there she was, next to her parents' headstone.

31

EPITAPH

SACRED TO THE MEMORY
OF EMILY MARY
THE BELOVED DAUGHTER OF
GEORGE AND EMILY KEELING
OF ARCH HILL

WHO WAS SHOT WHILE ON
HER WAY TO THE PRIMITIVE
METHODIST CHURCH
BIBLE-CLASS
ALEXANDRA STREET
APRIL 2ND 1886
AGED 17 YEARS.

THIS STONE WAS ERECTED BY
THE MEMBERS OF THE ABOVE
NAMED BIBLE-CLASS AND OTHER FRIENDS.

BE READY, MANY FALL AROUND
OUR LOVED ONES DISAPPEAR
WE KNOW NOT WHEN OUR CALL MAY COME
NOR SHOULD WE WAIT IN FEAR
IF READY, WE CAN CALMLY REST
LIVING OR DYING, WE ARE BLESSED.

The text was so pragmatic. There was no elaboration or attempt to disguise the tragedy of this death. More than one hundred years ago, a 17-year-old girl, on her way to church, was shot dead. What could possibly be the reason?

On the news page of the *New Zealand Herald* of 3 April 1886 I read the headline, "TRAGEDY AT ARCH HILL. MURDER AND SUICIDE. A YOUNG GIRL SHOT IN THE STREET". The language of the article expressed the horror at this crime:

> Shortly before seven o'clock yesterday evening a crime of a dreadful and tragic character was committed in Arch Hill, a young woman named Keeling being murdered in the public street by Edward Fuller, a rejected suitor for her hand, the murderer committing suicide in an adjoining street immediately after the perpetration of the deed.

"A rejected suitor". Edward loved Emily. Did Emily love Edward? I read on. Edward Fuller was 21 years old and had been living in New Zealand for three years. According to the paper, he had asked Emily's father for her hand in marriage two years earlier, and George Keeling had refused him on the grounds that Emily was too young. Edward lived with his sister just two houses away from the Keelings in King Street, and it was in this street, near the corner of New North Road, that the incident had occurred.

The story was also big news in the Saturday 3 April edition of the other Auckland newspaper at the time, the *Auckland Star*. "LOVE AND CRIME" read the headline. Included was a drawing of Emily Keeling and Edward Fuller. They looked like every drawing of every criminal and victim penned by last century's newspaper sketch artists: the faces are always impassive, and the features are regular and not drawn in any detail. But despite this, I fancied I could see something of a real Emily in her face.

She looked shy and sensible. She looked older than 17, but I am always struck by how serious and wise beyond their years young women looked last century. The *Star* stated Emily was of excellent character and had been popular. She was described as 'decidedly good looking, about medium height with blue eyes and brown hair'. Edward was drawn in profile and described as "a young man who has hitherto borne excellent character . . . He was between 21 and 22 years of age, about 5 feet 8 inches in height, of fair complexion, and moderate build. He did not wear a beard but had a light moustache." He was a labourer who had worked in the local brickyard.

In the next paragraph, I read that Emily's father, George, was a bricklayer by trade. I couldn't help but wonder if George and Edward might have worked together. Emily didn't work; she lived with her parents and looked after an 11-month-old foster brother. Emily had one older brother who lived in Brisbane. The birth dates of Emily's parents had been inscribed on their gravestone and from this I calculated George Keeling would have been 45 years old and Emily's mother, also called Emily, would have been 39 at the time.

The newspaper sketches of Emily and Edward.
NEWS MEDIA, FROM *AUCKLAND STAR*, 3 APR 1886

In the following day's edition of the *Herald*, the inquest was headline news, and details of Emily and Edward's story emerged. The local constable had found a suicide letter, written in red ink, in a pocket of the clothes Edward was wearing when he died. The letter was reprinted in full:

Dear brothers and sisters,
This will be the last time that I shall be able to write to you. When you have received this letter I shall be dead, as I am going to shoot myself to-night. Life is a misery to me now. I love Emily Keeling as no one ever loved before, and she cannot go with me because she is afraid her father would make a row again. If he had consented when I asked him the first time this would never have happened. I don't think she likes me so well now as she did then. It don't matter where I go I cannot stop and that is the reason I could not stop up at Henderson's Mill so I have made up my mind to shoot myself, as I cannot live without her. I shall speak to her tonight, and ask whether she will have me without her father's consent. If she objects we will both die together. You can divide my money between you and Lissia. So now I bid you all good-bye forever.
— from your loving brother, Ed. Jas. Fuller.

In the course of researching *Epitaph*, I have read a number of suicide notes and each time it gives me a very strange feeling. The clear, concise conviction of purpose is always there and is something I find quite chilling.

I was mystified, though, by Edward's reference to Henderson's Mill. But reading further I discovered a testimony made by Edward's brother-in-law Mr Jenkins, in which he said Edward had been working at a mill in the Northern Wairoa district for a year and a half and had returned to Auckland just after the Christmas of 1885. He couldn't bear to be away from Emily and he couldn't bear to be near her. Edward must have been struggling with these feelings for the two years since George Keeling forbade him to marry his daughter.

I had been staring into the bright screen of the library's microfilm reader for long enough. I sat back and reflected on all this. Edward and Emily. It could have been the story of many an innocent romance between two teenagers, and if it had ended as simply as so many of them do, I would never have known anything about either of them. But because of the tragic turn this story took, the lives of these two people and the little suburban street they lived in have been written up in exhaustive and emotive detail.

Arch Hill is a tiny suburb marooned by motorways and main roads. It was only two kilometres from the Symonds Street cemetery and about as much from the library. I quickly copied off the newspaper articles and headed back to the car. Before I drove off, I wanted to check something: Alexandra Street, where Emily was heading for her Bible class. I retrieved the Auckland street directory from the glove box and flipped to the A list. There was an Alexander Street but no Alexandra Street.

I found King Street easily enough, running off New North Road, which is now almost wall-to-wall car salesyards. A boldly striped takeaway bar marks the corner of King Street. Rounding the corner, I was struck by how King Street and the streets running off it remain very much as they must have been in Emily's time. The buildings are weatherboard, the roofs are iron, they have been built cheek by jowl on steep sections and almost all of them are perfect examples of the style of villa that is the signature of Auckland's oldest suburbs: a front porch, centred front door, two rooms either side of the corridor leading to the living area, which these days generally leads to an add-on out the back for the kitchen and bathroom.

Looking down the street, I wondered where Emily and Edward had lived. Could their houses still be here? I parked the car and spread the newspapers out on the seat next to me. The scene of the crime was described in great detail in the papers, and none of the street names given matched the names of streets that now ran off King Street. The report also talked about a store on the corner of one of the streets. According to my vague reckoning, I should have been parked directly outside it. There was no store there now, if I was in the right place. I would have to get my hands on some old city plans to find out which streets the 1886 reports were talking about. In the meantime I visited the Department of Statistics hoping to find out some more information on Emily's family. New Zealand has always kept very good records of our labour force, housing, education, etc., perhaps because a new colony was regarded as a great experiment, so needed careful monitoring. Even so, I was really impressed by what I found. I arrived at the Department of Statistics with a vague idea that I wanted some facts about family life in 1886. I found out a lot.

of George Keeling and John Jenkins. At the Department of Lands and Survey in the central city I was able to go back to old survey maps and try to match the property numbers I had found in the old electoral roles to the plots of land on the survey. I didn't really know what I was looking for since there were so many numbers listed on the plans and I didn't know which related to what. All I needed was a street number, which should have been straightforward enough, surely?

Talking to an official at the survey office, I soon discovered that there were no street numbers last century. So how did anything get delivered? Simply by name. Suburbs were communities where people knew each other and a name was enough to guide the postal service. With no corresponding street numbers to go by, it took me days of checking and cross referencing before I could be sure I had found the right houses. It was just as I had hoped. They were still there, just one house in between them, down the right-hand side of the street, only 100 metres from the corner of Dean Street where the store had been. But I found out something else that gave my heart a tug.

According to the conveyancing records, John Jenkins purchased a substantial plot of land in King Street in 1880. In 1881 he sold off two sections; the one directly next door he sold to a Hewitt family, and the section next to that to George Keeling. Keeling bought the property for 20 pounds. Emily would have been 12 years old. How inconceivable that George Keeling's choice of a property would have such dire consequences just five years later.

This must have been George's dream, to own freehold land, a possibility that would have seemed remarkable to a bricklayer. It was precisely this dream that lured people away from England, where private ownership was the preserve of the nobility. Arch Hill was a cheap inner-city suburb (on a steep south-facing hillside), and houses were built here for the labouring class. The land became available in the 1870s, as far as I could make out, and was bought up over the next few years. Today, most of the houses in King Street and in the streets around it are the very same homes built by these hard-working men and women as their first stake in a new life.

I still needed an old street map. So, off to the library. At the War Memorial Museum in Auckland there is a library on the fourth floor. Like the exhibits housed in the rest of the building, the library shows few signs of the passage of time. The old wooden shelves and polished wooden reading tables give the information found here an added air of authenticity. Every time I come here, I find other people also searching for clues about someone long gone but not forgotten.

I found an enormous map of the Newton area of Auckland. It contained answers to some of my questions: in particular, the paddock referred to by Emily in her second letter, and the mysterious street names. The newspaper article on the murder had reported Mr Thomas's store being on the corner of King and Stanley Streets. There was Stanley Street on the map exactly where I had pictured it in my mind. The street is still there but is now called Dean Street. The next corner, the place where Edward shot himself, was called Codrington Street and is known today as Potatau Street. This confirmed that the scenario, as I had pictured it, had indeed taken place exactly where I parked the car the day I went to see King Street for the first time.

According to the *New Zealand Herald* report, Emily set off up King Street, past Edward's house. She would have crossed the street and walked up toward New North

Road. Near the top of the street was a store on the corner of a small lane called Stanley Street. At this intersection, just above the store, Edward Fuller was waiting. He would have known Emily would be coming by for her regular Bible class, and must have left by his back door to avoid being seen by his or her family.

Emily's description of the paddock in her letter also made sense. The entire area between Ponsonby Road and Williamson Avenue, bordered in a sweeping arch by New North Road, was nothing but farmland. From the top of Emily's street, looking west along the route of

Emily's house as it is today (above) and Edward's almost next door (right).
PHOTOS: SIMON YOUNG

Ponsonby Road there would have been nothing but fields. This area was called Surrey Hills. Emily's city was very different from the one I was in now.

I turned my attention to the mystery of the location of Emily's church in Alexandra Street. In fact, it was easily solved. A call to the Methodist offices put me in contact with their archives department and the librarian knew exactly what I was referring to. Alexandra Street had been known as many things over the years and today it is called Airedale Street. The City Mission is still there. So this was the church that Emily and her family attended, the Methodist Church in the heart of the city, just opposite the Town Hall.

The inscription on Emily's headstone referred to "the primitive Methodist Church". What did this mean? Why was this church called primitive? What was different about this congregation? The Methodist Church offices sent me rafts of information in the post. The Primitive Methodists distinguished themselves from the Wesleyan Methodists in their style of worship and their working-class affiliations. The Primitives were very evangelical, often holding outdoor meetings. Their worshipping style was more spontaneous than the Wesleyans' and the congregation was distinctly more working-class. The church was often involved in workers' politics and provided leaders for labour movements. In its ideals and its style, this was the church of the labouring colonial.

Governor Grey had come into contact with the Primitive Methodists in Australia and had liked their "good works", so he donated them land in Auckland in Edwardes Street opposite the city's Town Hall. Edwardes Street became Alexandra Street. The church opened here in 1851 and would have provided a complete community. According to a copy of the original service timetable, there were meetings, events and services a dozen times a week. This was probably Emily's world.

In the 1880s, the social highlight of the week was wandering Queen Street late at night to view the illuminations and shop windows. The shops were open until ten o'clock, and people would meet and talk and enjoy being seen. Suddenly, my nine pm supermarket soirées didn't seem so revolutionary.

If the times then seemed a little restrictive in terms of excitement and opportunity, there was one matter in which they seemed disturbingly modern. Here was the story of a young man wielding a gun in the street. What was a quiet, homely 21-year-old doing with a gun?

A local gun-shop owner gave me the name of a friend who was an expert on guns. His name was Tony Dawe. We met and I gave him the newspaper report to read. Tony knew the gun described in the report: a British Bulldog 45 calibre. This meant it was powerful but slow. When it was fired, it had an enormous kick and produced a dense cloud of smoke. Where would Edward have got his hands on it? Well, that, it turned out, was the easiest part.

There were no gun laws anywhere until the twentieth century, when the Russian Revolution made governments fearful of an armed populace. Sports shops and gun shops stocked a wide range of pistols and rifles, and Edward would have only had to wander down Queen Street to choose from a number of stores. No questions would have been asked of him when he took his 12 pounds into a gun shop and bought the revolver and bullets. He had hunted before, for game up north, and like most young men he would have been familiar with a firearm. The Bulldog was a popular gun, mass-produced in Britain and Europe, and relatively cheap insurance in the days when your only defence was usually a weapon. The police, who were recruited from the Army, were not very conspicuous in early Auckland, and they could only come to you as fast as someone else could get to them to summon their assistance.

This was something of a revelation to me. I had always imagined early New Zealand city life being very quiet. Now, reading through the newspapers, I discovered it was full of mayhem, strife, vice and unexpected hurdles. We were a gun-carrying society. A society ready to defend itself when police numbers seemed impossibly inadequate. It seems bizarre we are still facing the same problem.

Though I found the ease with which Edward had got his hands on a firearm quite disturbing, I found something else that made him suddenly appear infinitely more dangerous. Nestled into the top of a neighbouring column of print in the report on the inquest, I discovered a letter submitted to the paper by a member of the jury. In it the juror stated his objection to the verdict of *Felo de se* or suicide. Instead he put forward a case for an insanity verdict. His grounds were these:

> Some two years ago the deceased young man, Fuller, fell passionately in love with a young woman he passed one day in the street. She resided in the Epsom district and for some time afterwards he used to be constantly following her about without being acquainted with her, without knowing her name, or without even knowing whether or not she was married.

The juror went on to state that Fuller "had worked himself into a state of morbid insanity recently, that for two or three days before Friday last he had neither washed himself nor combed his hair, although under ordinary circumstances he was very particular as to his personal appearance and adornment".

Edward had stalked a complete stranger without knowing anything about her. His relationship with her existed only in his own head. Unrequited passions and controlling obsessions were characteristic, it seemed, of Edward's dealings with women. Emily would have had no idea of the enormity of emotional feeling Edward had sustained over the years with little encouragement from her. A quiet young man living in the suburbs reappeared in my mind as a recluse who lived in a fantasy world.

In the Heritage section of the Public Library, I found a couple of photographs of Arch Hill from the 1880s. The roads are unsealed and houses are evidently springing up over the hills that are still just apparent. There was no street lighting as far out as New North Road, and as Arch Hill was technically outside the city limits then, there was no public transport. What amazed me was that at seven o'clock on an April evening, when it was already dark, Emily intended to walk from her home in King Street, all the way along New North Road to Karangahape Road, then along K. Road to Queen Street and down to the church. She must have made this journey hundreds of times before. On this night, she left her house at 20minutes to seven. She would have said goodbye to her mother and probably cuddled her baby brother and called out a goodbye to her father.

Arch Hill in the 1880s (below and right). AUCKLAND CITY LIBRARIES 5262; (RIGHT) 764

According to witnesses of the murder, Emily walked straight past Edward when she came upon him on the Stanley Street corner, but he reached out and grabbed her by the arm. The two exchanged words, but no one heard what was said. Suddenly, there was a loud bang followed by another and Emily staggered backwards. She had been shot twice in the chest at close range.

The shots were heard by a woman who had just walked past the couple and by the storekeeper Mr Thomas, who was in his living room next to the store. As Thomas ran outside, Emily was running towards him and cried, 'Oh, save me!' He told her to go to his store. Edward turned and ran past them on the other side of the road, up Stanley Street. Thomas immediately turned his attention to Emily who was collapsed on the front steps of the shop. "I am shot. Save me. Take me in," is what Thomas heard her say. He and his son carried Emily into their front room and laid her on their sofa. She was conscious and distressed. Mr Thomas's son ran to get a doctor and Mrs Thomas undid Emily's dress and took off her boots and gloves. Outside people were gathering in the street having heard the shots and the screams. A neighbour ran to get Emily's parents.

Some locals found Edward's body lying face down in a pool of blood on the corner of Stanley Street and Codrington Street. A gun was in his right hand, his thumb, not his finger on the trigger guard. A young boy ran to get a policeman, who arrived on the scene at five minutes to seven. At this point, the police and the men who had found Edward had no idea he had just shot Emily Keeling at the other end of the street.

Emily knew she would not survive. "Love me, I am dying," she said to Mrs Thomas. Mrs Thomas replied, "Yes darling, I will. God bless you." Mrs Thomas then asked Emily

*Mr Thomas's store, outside which
Emily was fatally shot.* NEWS MEDIA, *AUCKLAND STAR*
COLLECTION, 3 APR 1886

who had shot her and she replied, "Ted Fuller did it." Emily's parents arrived but there was nothing more anyone could do.

Dr Lawson from Karangahape Road arrived just after seven o'clock. Emily was only moments from death. She had been shot in her left lung and was gasping for breath. At quarter past seven, Emily died. Her body was carried to her parents' house.

I felt shattered reading the story of the actual murder. It was a slow death, a calculated murder. Emily was young, it was a life lost before it had really been lived: "We know not when our call may come."

The tragedy caught Auckland up in a wave of mourning. People turned out to give Emily Keeling the largest funeral the city had ever seen. Following the route Emily walked so often, the funeral procession left her home in King Street at three o'clock on the Saturday afternoon. Dense crowds lined the streets, particularly from Ponsonby Road, along Karangahape Road and at the entrance to the cemetery. The newspapers numbered the crowd at 10,000 people. I knew from my forays at the Statistics Department that the population of Auckland at the time was only 35,000. It was quite incredible.

Heading the procession were members of the Alexandra Street Sunday School. Behind them came the hearse and then the mourning carriage bearing George and Emily Keeling and two female friends. Then followed a long line of young women marching three abreast, then a group of young men. They were members of the Bible class and friends of the family. The procession of the general public followed with the crowds falling in behind as it passed.

At the cemetery, the coffin had to be carried down the steep slope through the crowds to the gravesite. Mrs Keeling was so distraught she had to be supported, and the minister of the Alexandra Street Methodist Church took the service "with more than ordinary feeling". Friends threw garlands of flowers into the open grave and then dispersed, leaving Emily and George Keeling to make their way home with a few close friends.

Where Edward Fuller is buried I cannot be sure. I contacted all the cemeteries that were open in Auckland at the time but none of them have any record of Edward's burial. Because the verdict was suicide, he would have been placed in an unmarked grave.

I wondered what happened to the Keelings after this. Emily, it seemed, had been their life, particularly for her mother. In the conveyance records there is mention of the sale of the Keelings' property in 1902. Jenkins continued to live almost next door, and his son inherited the property.

There was one last mystery. Something that had been nagging at me since my first reading of the paper reports. There was something most unusual about the Keelings' fostering a baby. It was a foster son and Emily looked after it. The baby appeared in the family about six months after Edward left to go up north. Why would parents of adult children take on a baby? Mrs Keeling said the child was fostered. She never signed any adoption papers for the child and when I found the baby Keeling's birth certificate it stated that his name was Harry and his parents were Emily and George Keeling. The names of birth parents are usually on the birth certificate and the names of later parents would be listed on adoption papers. Who was Harry Keeling? While her parents Emily and George Keeling share Emily's grave, nothing more is known of Harry Keeling or the "illness" that confined Emily to bed when she wrote Edward the first letter. Perhaps it is better that way.

*blivion*

JOHANNA'S STORY WAS REVEALED in a most unusual way. Often an epitaph demands attention. Inscriptions can be heart-wrenching, compelling, bizarre and secretive. Sometimes it is the lonely grave that draws us, sometimes it is a grave that seems out of place. In Johanna's case it was something quite different. Johanna's epitaph doesn't yield any clues about her life. There is nothing out of the ordinary about her grave. But Johanna's story reached out and demanded to be told. One hundred years after she died, a stranger was inexplicably drawn to her grave and so began a search that would take years.

Barry Shaw who takes guided walking tours around Waikumete Cemetery happened to mention to me one day that there was one particular very old grave that was regularly and lavishly tended. Barry had spoken to the man looking after the grave and knew that he was not a relative, nor was he connected to the woman buried there in any way. This intrigued me. Why would a stranger take the time to look after the grave of a woman he had never known and to whom he owed nothing?

I finally met Roy Kellett, the mystery man tending Johanna's grave, only to discover there were no simple answers to these questions. According to Roy, he was walking through Waikumete Cemetery one day in 1986, and felt drawn to one of the graves. Under a tree, and slightly set apart from the other graves, was an overgrown headstone bearing the name Johanna McCarthy. Roy had often walked past here, but on this particular day he felt as if he was being physically drawn to the grave. He dismissed the feeling at first but then decided to look at the grave.

> JOHANNA MCCARTHY
> Co. KERRY. IRELAND.
> THE BELOVED WIFE OF
> GEORGE BINNING
> WHO DIED APRIL 17TH 1886
> AGED 37 YEARS
> MAY SHE REST IN PEACE

I was struck by the date: 17 April 1886. Johanna must have been buried at Waikumete because the Grafton cemetery had just closed after the burial of Emily Keeling two weeks earlier. Surely Johanna knew about Emily's murder; a young woman shot on her way to Bible class by a man who was determined they should be together, in death if not in life. Emily's funeral attracted 10,000 people; perhaps Johanna was there. She too would have been struck by the tragedy of Emily Keeling's death. Could she have had any inkling that her own death was just two weeks away?

From the first moment he saw Johanna's grave, Roy says he knew there was a tragic story buried with this woman. All he had was her name and the date of her death. This would be the beginning of Roy's search and the interweaving of two lives separated by a century. Roy became Johanna's biographer and friend. He spent years meticulously cross-referencing records and reports: death certificates, marriage records, adoption agencies, electoral roles, passenger lists, even weather reports. It is only because of Roy's tenacious and faithful work that Johanna's story can be told.

Johanna's immigration echoes that of thousands of women who came out to New Zealand, sure that there would be a better life here. When she arrived in Auckland in December 1863, she was only 14 or 15 years old. By then she had already lived a difficult life, shared by the thousands who suffered in the Irish Potato Famine of the 1840s. Born in County Kerry, Johanna had grown up in one of the most dramatically and ruggedly beautiful places in the world. The southwest heel of Ireland is fingered with peninsulas, it is rocky and grand and wild. But when potato crops began to fail, the whole of Ireland was plunged into one of the darkest chapters in its history. By 1850, more than one and a half million people were dead. Johanna's parents were among them.

Johanna left Ireland in the company of Thomas and Catherine O'Sullivan, who had adopted her. The three of them took the ferry from Cork to Falmouth, then the train to London, bringing them to their ship, the *Bombay*, which sailed from England in August 1863.

*T*he Bombay, *the ship Johanna sailed on to come to New Zealand.* ALEXANDER TURNBULL LIBRARY C9587

Ship diaries give us brief glimpses into the experiences of New Zealand's early immigrants, and by all accounts the voyage of the *Bombay* was a pleasant one. Compared with the food available in Ireland, the meals aboard ship were evidently generous. The highlight of that voyage must have been the birth of Catherine O'Sullivan's daughter, Mary Agatha.

Perhaps just coincidentally, Roy and his family arrived in New Zealand in 1963, exactly 100 years after Johanna. Roy had flown in the RAF during the Second World War and was based in Ireland. He knew the Irish landscape well and the seas around its coast. Johanna's journey out is very clear in his mind. Roy's family settled in Henderson in West Auckland.

The O'Sullivans bought a small farm near the new settlement of Avondale. Everyone was a new chum. There was no such thing as a "local". People from all over Britain and from Australia and many other countries in Europe were digging in together and trying to get on in life. Families, couples, men and women were streaming out to the colony and establishing homes and towns on freshly broken land without any of the facilities even famine-decimated Ireland could provide.

Johanna worked on the farm for a while but then left and made her way to Thames. Only a ferry ride from Auckland, Thames was built on the promise of gold, and by the 1870s its population had swelled to 1800 in a rush that was to make this goldfield famous worldwide. When Johanna arrived there she would have found herself in a thriving, chaotic and sprawling town that had grown almost overnight into the third largest centre in the country.

Despite the population size, life was basic. Joanna would have lived without running water and probably joined the rest of the women doing a weekly wash in the Karaka Stream. The cottages had mud floors and thousands of men were living in tents. One thing I had never considered about life in a mining town was the noise. Gold batteries were used to crush the rock in which the gold was trapped, and in Thames there were more than 500 stampers creating a thunderous noise that continued night and day, stopping only on Sundays. A curious problem arose when the public began complaining that it was too quiet on Sunday to sleep!

There were a lot of banks and hotels and plenty of work. It's quite likely Johanna worked in one of the hotel bars, which were a gathering place for everyone seeking respite from a day of hard labour. Perhaps it was here she met George Binning. Before the gold strikes, the Coromandel Peninsula was famous for its kauri logging and gum digging. Kauri gum was in high demand for the preparation of linoleum, varnish and dental supplies. George Binning was a gum digger.

George was born in England and, like Johanna, had lived in New Zealand since he was a teenager. George and Johanna were married on 22 June 1872 in Benjamin Gahner's private residence in Karaka. They were both 22 years old. The private wedding must have meant the couple's religious differences prevented them being married in a church, and in death they were still separate — Johanna lies in the Roman Catholic part of Waikumete Cemetery, George in the Anglican. In marrying him, Johanna had defied the principles of her faith.

Within months of their marriage, Johanna and George adopted a part-Maori girl and named her Nellie. Was this an attempt by Johanna to repeat her own good fortune in being adopted into a loving family after losing her own? At this point during her life in Thames, the scent goes cold and it's not till many years later, once they had moved back to Auckland, that we are able to pick up the trail again. We know Johanna and Nellie were living in Parnell in what is now called Tilden Street. George was working as a slaughterman at a butcher's in Ellerslie and came home only on Saturdays. A journey that takes 15 to 20 minutes by car was, in 1885, a long horse-and-cart ride for George and necessitated living near his work. It also seems that he had virtually "cleared out", as Johanna put it. So, somewhere between marrying the man of her dreams in Thames and the mid-1880s where we find Johanna back in Auckland, her life had changed dramatically. From the hope and promise of her early 20s she was now coping with a broken marriage and raising the difficult Nellie on her own.

On 10 March 1886, Nellie appeared in court charged with stealing a watch worth 35 shillings. She was remanded and stayed in the cells for three days.

George Binning later said that after Nellie's involvement with the law, Johanna started to deteriorate. She began seeing things moving around the house and became physically unwell. Today Johanna's behaviour would have been diagnosed as a nervous breakdown. She was 37 years old and had no one to turn to: her husband apparently wasn't prepared to act like a husband; her daughter who wasn't her daughter had shamed her; and the country she lived in wasn't her original home.

She became very ill. George called a doctor to attend to Johanna on Tuesday 13 April. The doctor sent George out to get medicine and told him to get Johanna a nurse. The doctor's advice was clear: Johanna should not be left alone. George told the inquest that he did get a nurse but the very next morning Johanna left the house in Tilden Street.

The closest friends she had in the world were her adoptive parents, Thomas and Catherine O'Sullivan. It must have been with a heavy heart that she took the Wednesday morning train to Avondale with Nellie to stay with them. This was on 14 April. Johanna confided in the O'Sullivans that she couldn't see any possible future and wanted to kill herself. The O'Sullivans must have been horrified. Now in their 60s, Thomas and Catherine had acted as parents to Johanna for more than 20 years and the three of them had been through a lot together.

Johanna and Nellie stayed in Avondale that night and returned to Auckland the next day. They arrived at the Queen Street station at dusk. It wasn't a particularly pleasant evening. Weather reports from the day's papers describe a typical grey April evening with rain expected and a cold nor'easterly blowing in off the harbour. Johanna must have been thinking about what she was going to do. From Queen Street train station, Johanna took Nellie to the nearest police station.

There were two officers on duty there that night. The report in the newspaper on 17 April, the day after her death, relayed the conversation Johanna had with the officers:

[She] requested Mounted-constable Kelly to take charge of the child as she could do nothing with her, and if he did not she would make away with herself. Sergeant Pratt entered the guard room and the unfortunate woman renewed her request, stating she wanted him to take the child over, as the father had cleared out, and she could look after her no longer. Sergeant Pratt said she had come rather late, and advised her to return in the morning, when he would see what could be done for her.

Johanna left the police station with Nellie, and the two were next seen a couple of hours later by Johanna's good friend Rosa Erte. They arrived at Rosa's house in Eden Street at about 9.30, and Johanna asked if they could stay the night. Rosa put Johanna into a room in the house next door, which she also owned. Johanna lay down on the bed fully clothed at about quarter to 10. When Rosa went to check on her just after 10 o'clock, she was gone.

Auckland wharf in the 1880s. ALEXANDER TURNBULL LIBRARY F2195 1/2

At 7.30 the next morning, a man working at the Devonport Ferry Company noticed something lying underneath one of the ships in their slipyard. It had been left by the high tide. When the man realised it was a woman's body, he sent for the police. The woman had no shoes on and was lying stretched out on the shore, her left hand lying across her heart. It was Johanna.

Roy and I walked together, following the route that Johanna must have taken on the night she died. Leaving Rosa Erte's house, she would have made her way down Hobson Street toward the docks. A casino, a television station and a large liquormart now line the route. In 1886 the street was full of houses. It wasn't the best part of town, and I was curious as to why Rosa happened to own more than one house in the area. It could have been that they were "establishments" where women worked: brothels. Perhaps Rosa was an acquaintance from Johanna's Thames days? Female orphans from poor families had few options last century, and it is possible that, rather than be a burden on the O'Sullivans, Johanna had supported herself in Thames by working as a prostitute. Perhaps Nellie really was her daughter; certainly George would have seemed like the answer to her dreams if he had taken her away from that life. But we will never know.

When Johanna reached Customs Street, she would have seen the Custom House and the Ferry Building looming darkly on her right. Ahead of her were shipyards, a brickworks, the morgue building and boats up on the hard, where they were cleaned and repaired, and moored in the tide.

> A few more steps to the jetty
> tall ships and steamers creaking and groaning
> in the strong northeast window
> Clouds scudding in the dark night sky
> the sea cold, black and heaving
> below her stocking feet.
> Hesitation now, the reality is there
> 'Oblivion'
> One step forward
> a plunge into darkness
> and the cold dark heaving sea
> envelops Johanna.

This is one section of a poem Roy wrote some time ago when he was thinking about those last moments of Johanna's life. She wouldn't have been able to swim. It was very rare in the 1800s to find anyone who could swim, and death by drowning was horribly common. Barely a day goes by in the newspapers of the time when drownings are not reported.

The constable who arrived on the scene that morning confirmed there were no marks of violence on Johanna's body and ordered it to be taken to the morgue, which was only metres away on Customs Street West. George Binning and Rosa Erte both came to identify the body.

Johanna's wedding ring and 'keeper' (a plain ring worn to keep a valuable ring on the same finger from being lost) were found wrapped in a piece of paper in one of her pockets; and a rather unusual find was made behind the morgue. In a neat pile under two large stones lay Johanna's shawl, a pair of boots and a black hat. Whoever had placed them there had done so carefully, making sure the wind wouldn't carry the clothes away.

An inquest was held that afternoon in a nearby hotel, attended by a jury, a coroner, a doctor and a police constable. Fortunately, a post-mortem wasn't considered necessary. In those days, the jury (all men) observed the post-mortem. Even if a body was exhumed, the jury was expected to be present when the body was removed from the grave.

In this case the verdict read, 'That the deceased was found drowned without marks of violence'. It's a verdict open to interpretation and was a euphemistic description of what was obviously a suicide. Johanna had told her adoptive parents that she wanted to kill herself. She had told the police that she intended to take her own life. No one had taken her despair seriously.

Roy has scrubbed Johanna's headstone. Fresh flowers are often laid at the grave. Decorative shells are patterned on the ground. One day Johanna's headstone toppled over and it took six people to raise it upright again. The monument is made from solid marble, which is unusual. Marble was the preserve of the wealthy, and it is unlikely George Binning would have had the money to commemorate Johanna in such style.

Sure enough, Roy discovered looking through the cemetery records that the headstone had been paid for by Thomas O'Sullivan in 1893. This might account for the discrepancy in the date of Johanna's death and the date carved on her stone. She died on 16 April but it is recorded in her epitaph as the 17th. It's a small inaccuracy, but searching back through written accounts more than 100 years old, I find that mistakes were common, making it harder to uncover the true facts. That the O'Sullivans paid for the gravestone might also account for Johanna being buried with her maiden name. Perhaps the decision not to use her married name was a sign of the O'Sullivans' feelings toward George Binning.

Johanna's name was at the top of the list of burials at Waikumete for 1886; she was the first Catholic to be buried there. The only strange thing about this find is that it was almost unheard of for a woman who had committed suicide to be buried on consecrated ground with a memorial stone. Added to this was the comment made in the cemetery records by the priest who buried her, Walter McDonald. In the margins of the book, he had penned in fine scrawl, "So glad to see my old friend." It was a very curious remark. What could it mean?

Walter McDonald was also Irish and arrived in New Zealand in 1855. He was ordained as a priest a year later. He became the priest at St Patrick's Cathedral and was later appointed the private secretary to Bishop Pompallier. He was even made chaplain of the racing club in an effort by the Church to rein in the wayward spirits of the local jockeys and punters. Father McDonald was later appointed a monsignor by the Pope for his services to the Church.

Father McDonald must have known Johanna — the residents of Parnell were his "flock". He walked a lot, carrying sweets for the children in his pockets. He spoke fluent Maori and was admired for the respect he accorded everyone regardless of their faith or standing.

History books recall him as a "Victorian gentleman", and when he died on the last day of the last year of last century, "persons of all creeds and classes felt as though they

Roy at Johanna's grave holding a piece of coral he found buried by the headstone — was this to symbolise her death at sea? PHOTO: SIMON YOUNG

had lost a friend who had worthily won their love and esteem". His funeral procession was more than a mile long and included 120 carriages and 50 other vehicles. It was truly the end of an era.

For everything that I had discovered about Father McDonald and as much as I felt an enormous warmth towards the man, I still had no idea what his comment may have meant — "So glad to see my old friend."

The other people in Johanna's life died soon after her or just disappeared. George Binning contracted bovine tuberculosis in 1889 and is buried at Waikumete in an unmarked grave. There is absolutely no trace of Nellie Binning. On George's death certificate no wife or children are listed. If Nellie had been formally adopted and was still alive in 1889, she should have been mentioned. However, she isn't mentioned on Johanna's death certificate either. Records for adoption in these years are incomplete and many informal adoptions took place. There are no marriage records for Nellie — she just vanished.

The O'Sullivans are both buried at Waikumete. Their daughter, Mary Agatha, married an Irishman and had at least two children. Rosa Erte might never have existed for all I knew, if she hadn't given a statement at the inquest into Johanna's death. There are no marriage or death records for her and she is not listed in the 1886 directory.

Roy still can't explain why he felt so drawn to Johanna's grave, but thanks to him, Johanna has, ironically, outlived them all. She is like a member of Roy's family. Everyone talks about her and the whole family visits the grave. Johanna lost her first family and left the second, but now she has a third.

51

The Confessions of a Cold-blooded Killer

WHILE VISITING THE WEST Coast, like thousands before me I had stopped at the Hokitika lookout simply to appreciate the fine view of the township below, the wild shoreline and the Tasman sea beyond. As I got out of my car, I noticed a memorial stone. This is not an unusual sight round there, but closer inspection sparked a search that would lead me on the path of four of our country's most notorious mass murderers.

The inscription revealed that it was a memorial to four government workers who had been killed in the course of their work. Three had been drowned, but for the fourth, George Dobson, the inscription read:

GEORGE DOBSON, ROAD ENGINEER,
MURDERED ON THE GREY AND ARNOLD ROAD,
MAY 28, 1866

George Dobson, road engineer: I had never heard of him, but someone cared enough to erect a memorial in this windswept place. By simply asking around the area, it didn't take me long to find out that George came from a famous family who tended to get their names on things — big things. The Dobson River was named after his father and Arthur's Pass after his brother. And the West Coast township of Dobson was named after George himself. He was killed just outside the town itself, where another memorial marks the actual spot:

SACRED TO THE MEMORY OF GEORGE DOBSON C.E.
GOVERNMENT ENGINEER— MURDERED HERE BY
BUSHRANGERS, 28 MAY, 1866.

Bushrangers! In New Zealand? I had been brought up on the tales of Ned Kelly, Australian bushranger, but I had never heard of any local versions.

After asking around in Dobson, I found out that our friend Mr Dobson the engineer was murdered by the most notorious gang of psychopaths ever known in New Zealand: the Burgess Gang, otherwise known as the Maungatapu Murderers. This latter name referred to the fact that George was not the gang's only victim, and, as I was to discover, not their first.

A glance at my map revealed that Maungatapu (or Sacred Mountain) was very near Nelson, and my investigations soon led me to the Nelson Museum, which holds an extensive collection of artefacts and memorabilia about the Burgess Gang. Chief among these are the death masks of three of the killers: Richard Burgess, Thomas Kelly, and Phillip Levy. There is no mask for the fourth, and some say the most dangerous, member of the band, Joseph Sullivan, because he escaped the hangman's noose. Holding these masks, knowing they were made from the faces of three dead killers, gave me an eerie feeling. But it also made me want to know more about the men who killed George Dobson, and many more.

The newspapers of the time provided plenty of sensational background to the case, but I soon discovered an unexpected, remarkable source of information: the words of Richard Burgess himself — 50,000 of them, to be precise — for Burgess wrote the story of his life while he was awaiting trial for murder in Nelson Gaol. The memoirs are a step-by-step account of the gang's murderous progress, and provided a chilling insight into the mind of a cold-blooded killer.

In his memoirs, Burgess tried to exonerate Kelly and Levy, and, while admitting his own murderous nature, said that Sullivan was guilty of several murders, including that of George Dobson. Sullivan, who had turned Queen's evidence and dobbed his fellow gang members in, naturally told a different story in the dock. Burgess, Kelly and Levy were all killers, he said; but not he — he had only ever been a lookout.

No one will ever know just where the truth lies, but because Burgess wrote his version down, his voice speaks most strongly from the grave:

Selecting the West Coast as a field to carry out my nefarious pursuits, I must needs confess it that my plans were bloody.

The gold rushes of the 1860s were perfect for someone like Burgess. It was like the Wild West, as droves of men, and a few women, from all over the world poured into Otago, Canterbury and the West Coast. As well as honest fortune-seekers came professional gamblers, sly groggers and brothel keepers — and outright criminals. Among the worst of them was Burgess — a Londoner who had been transported as a convict to Tasmania. His name was originally Richard Hill, but he had changed it to avoid detection, as he, by his own admission, had murdered four men in Australia before bolting to New Zealand.

Richard Burgess
NELSON PROVINCIAL MUSEUM

Burgess arrived in New Zealand in Dunedin, where he teamed up with another Londoner with a villainous background, Irishman Thomas Noon (later known as Kelly). Burgess and Noon began in Gabriel's Gully in 1862 as legitimate prospectors, but soon worked out that there was a much easier way to get gold, by robbing other prospectors. They did this at night, choking their victims into unconsciousness before robbing them. But one victim was not choked quickly enough, called out for help, and the pair were caught and sentenced to three years in Dunedin Gaol.

During this time, many others made legitimate fortunes in the "Shotover Rush", but by the time the pair were released, the rush was over and the gold had been worked out. But there was a new rush starting in Hokitika, so only four days after leaving prison in 1865, the two set off for the West Coast, travelling over Arthur's Pass, which had been discovered by Arthur Dobson the year before.

Burgess and Noon had been followed by police for some time on their release, but had managed to give them the slip. To their dismay, however, when they arrived in Hokitika they were recognised by a policeman who had been in the arresting party at Gabriel's Gully. So they were forced to behave as legitimate miners, and they staked a claim five miles inland from Hokitika, at the Kanieri River.

Thomas Noon (Kelly)
NELSON PROVINCIAL MUSEUM

Here, Noon took out his mining licence in the false name of Kelly, and was known as that from then onwards. The pair worked honestly as miners for two months until the police lost interest in them. They had some success at mining, but soon returned to the easier task of stealing gold. Burgess and Kelly went on a Christmas spree, committing more than 20 robberies at Hokitika. Even after splashing out on riotous living, Burgess was left with 500 pounds at the end of the holidays.

To all intents and purposes a successful miner, he bought a house at Hokitika and moved in with his girlfriend, a woman named Carrie. Burgess employed someone to work his diggings at Kanieri, while he and Kelly roamed the West Coast in search of more easy pickings.

Burgess soon tired of small-time theft, and also needed more money to support Carrie, who was soon pregnant with his child. Strangely for someone who killed so easily, Burgess had some moral scruples. He wanted the child to be born legitimately and so planned to marry Carrie. But he could not do so under his false name of Burgess, nor could he use his real name Hill, as this would have prompted the local police to obtain his criminal records from Melbourne.

*P*hilip Levy
NELSON PROVINCIAL MUSEUM

So, he began to think big, hatching a plan to rob the banks at Okarito, marry Carrie in Sydney, then escape to Europe with thousands of pounds and live like royals. In case the plan failed, he gave her the house and most of his remaining cash — 370 pounds.

For such an ambitious plan as the Okarito banks, he needed a bigger gang, and soon recruited two other Londoners with criminal backgrounds: Philip Levy and Joseph Sullivan. Levy was a gold-buyer and small-time fence for stolen goods whom Burgess and Kelly had known in Dunedin, and Sullivan was a former prize-fighter whom Kelly had known slightly at school in London. Sullivan had also known Levy in the Otago goldfields, where some later claimed they had killed up to 20 diggers for their gold.

Burgess, although the youngest at 36, was clearly the leader of the gang and made all the major decisions. His plan was for them to rob the banks disguised as policemen, so he raided the police camp at Hokitika, stealing two police revolvers with holsters, ammunition belts and riding breeches — but unfortunately for him no police hats or tunics. The police were enraged and began to search all known criminals'

*J*oseph Sullivan
NELSON PROVINCIAL MUSEUM

houses. In order to explain how he had two guns, should they be found, Burgess hid them on the beach, then staged "finding" them while he was out walking with the local publican.

So, when Burgess was arrested for having the holsters under his bed, he had a solid citizen as a witness to say that he had found them. The magistrate was obliged to drop the charges of theft, but the local paper, influenced by the police, made a meal out of the case. They published his caricature, with details of his arrest and imprisonment in Dunedin, and hints of his nefarious doings around the West Coast.

This put paid to Burgess's plan to rob the Okarito banks, and soon the local police told him and Kelly to clear out of town. They did so, with Sullivan travelling half a mile behind them, carrying a swag containing the gang's ammunition, Burgess's two revolvers and his own shotgun.

The three ended up in Greymouth, where they met Levy, who had travelled up by boat — apparently the dandy of the group, he took pains not to be seen in company with the others, who looked more like criminals.

In Greymouth, Sullivan began a drinking bout which soaked up what little money they had left. Desperate for funds, they agreed a job had to be pulled, and decided to rob a local gold-buyer, Edwin Fox.

What happened next, no one outside the gang knows for certain. Sullivan swore that three of them took part; Burgess swears that Sullivan and another man did it. But it seems fairly certain that Sullivan, at least, mistook Dobson for Fox and accosted him on the road eight miles out of Greymouth. At first, Dobson must have thought he was in no danger, as Sullivan allegedly told Burgess, "He laughed and said: 'Did you take me for a banker? Here is all the money I have, six pounds odd.'"

"He was such a nice young fellow too," Sullivan said, "But I couldn't let him pass because he had seen me without any disguise. So I took him into the scrub about a hundred yards from the road. I made him sit down and there we burked him. I raked a hole and put him in it compass and all."

Dobson's death by strangulation and the 6 pounds it gained didn't solve the gang's financial problems. But they had bigger plans, for as Burgess wrote in his memoirs, the banks of the West Coast of the South Island were entirely at the mercy of any marauders who liked to enter them.

Their first attempt at a bank job failed, for the simple reason that there was no bank to rob. When the gang was travelling north on the steamer from Greymouth to Nelson, Burgess, Kelly and Sullivan went ashore at Westport armed with revolvers to rob the bank there. But, to their disgust, they had been misinformed. There was no bank. They rushed back aboard, and had to borrow the fare from Levy to travel on to Nelson. Here they disembarked, with only a few shillings between them, but armed to the teeth with two revolvers, two double-barrelled shotguns and a variety of knives. As well, Sullivan (or Levy, according to Sullivan) had a bottle containing enough strychnine to poison 100 people.

The gang decided to make for the Wakamarina goldfield, where they intended to carry on their well-practised habit of robbing, and killing if necessary. To get to the goldfield, they had to travel on foot along a pack-horse track up the Matai Valley over the Maungatapu Track to a place called Canvastown — so called because of the large number of miners' tents there. They had to trudge up over Mt Maungatapu and spent their first night near the summit beside a large rock where the views are stunning. But Richard Burgess wasn't looking at the scenery. His memoirs revealed that when he first saw the place, he thought:

> This would be a good place to stick up any travellers along this track. We could do them over and plant their bodies in the bush in these ferny gullies. They'd never be found.

They arrived in Canvastown the following day, where a local storekeeper named Jervis, thinking they were miners down on their luck, let them stay in an empty hut. The gangsters repaid him by stealing two of his hens and a cabbage from his garden. There looked to be slim pickings in Canvastown, so Levy was sent on by the gang to nearby Deep Creek to see if there was any loot to be had there. He soon returned with news that a group of businessmen were about to close up shop and move their cash and gold to the bank in Nelson. The gang promptly decided to rob and murder them on the Maungatapu Track. In Burgess's own words:

> If they never turn up at Nelson no one will know the difference. We must put up these blokes.

The little hut became a hive of murderous industry. Burgess borrowed a whetstone from Jervis to sharpen his knives. They cleaned and oiled the shotguns and the revolvers. The following morning, to throw suspicion off themselves, they left in the opposite direction to Nelson but doubled back. As they left, Jervis called out goodbye to them, and Burgess shouted in reply, "We are going to leave this bloody place, there is nothing to do here."

The men from Deep Creek had also left for Nelson the same morning. In the party were two storekeepers, John Kempthorne and James Dudley, hotelkeeper Felix Mathieu and miner James de Pontius. They had a pack-horse with them and carried gold and money totalling 300 pounds. They reached Canvastown about noon and left for Nelson that afternoon, staying overnight at an inn, and starting out on the Maungatapu Track the next morning. This would be their last day on earth; but they were not to be the gang's only victims that morning.

As the bushrangers moved along the track, they were passed by a 54-year-old flax-cutter known as Jamie Battle. They exchanged greetings and let him pass, but the gang suddenly realised that he was a potential witness to what they intended, and Sullivan and Burgess rushed after him. Battle realised that he was in danger and drew a knife, but the pair overcame him and dragged him off the track into the bush.

"If you murder me, I shall be foully murdered," he cried, just before Burgess began to choke him.

Burgess later wrote:

A sketch of Jamie Battle's murder as imagined by the papers at the time. ALEXANDER TURNBULL LIBRARY F316 35MM A

I took him by the throat and held him till he was dead, his livid eyes and blackened face staring at me as if to say look at your handiwork.

But Burgess's work was less than handy that day. Battle was not yet dead, and Sullivan finished the job — or so he thought, with a terrible blow to the stomach. They picked up Jamie's shovel, dug a shallow hole, rolled him in and covered him with dirt and ferns. It was a botched job, and medical evidence would later show that Battle was still alive when buried.

Sullivan remarked to Burgess:

That's not the way that I burke a man; the next we do, I'll show you my way.

To "burke" a man meant to stab or strangle him; the word comes from an earlier murderer — the notorious Burke — who, along with Hare, dug up bodies and killed strangers to sell to the medical students at Edinburgh University.

Battle's murder had netted just 3 pounds 17 shillings. But much more was to come. They soon reached the area around the large rock which ever since has been known as "Murderers' Rock". The gang cleared scrub nearby and put up dead branches to hide behind, and also made paths to get the bodies off the track. They prepared straps and sashes to tie their victims. At one point, their work was interrupted when a couple, a man and a woman, approached along the track. The gangsters hid in the bushes, and Sullivan apparently favoured killing them also. But Burgess had some scruples and insisted on letting them pass, saying, "We have had mothers and sisters of our own."

The Deep Creek party finally arrived, and (again, depending on whose version of events you believe) Burgess and Sullivan emerged with guns ready. Burgess yelled, "Stand, bail up!" while Kelly moved in to block their escape. The men were bound and led some distance off the track, and were told that they would be released later. This was a lie, as Burgess later wrote that the night before he had decided "We would burke the whole lot of them."

The victims were separated and the gang began their grisly work. Dudley was the first to die, strangled by Sullivan within earshot of the others, who immediately began to scream and shout. The robbers abandoned the strangling idea, and shot Kempthorne and de Pontius. Mathieu died the hardest; he was shot, stabbed with a sheaf knife and shot again. Even the horse wasn't spared. After taking the money off it, they shot it as well. Although the bodies were hidden well off the track, de Pontius was the only one they buried, figuring that, if the other bodies were discovered, he would be seen as the guilty party.

Even Burgess believed that what they had done "cannot be paralleled in atrocity". But the killers were not weighed down by conscience. They moved up the track and built a fire, where they burnt incriminating letters and papers in the dead men's swags. They divvied up the cash before moving on to Nelson where they sold the stolen gold.

Each murderer got 80 pounds, not enough for their life of leisure in Europe, but at a time when honest working men earned only 2 or 3 pounds in a week, it was very good money for a few days' walk in the bush. Anxious to clear the area as soon as possible, the gang found that they couldn't get a ship out of Nelson for a week. Still, having concealed their crimes, they were confident enough to go shopping for new clothes. And Burgess amused himself by going riding with the local publican and his daughter.

The killers had counted on no one missing the men they had murdered for a week or two. But, unknown to them, the Deep Creek party had arranged for a friend named Moller to follow them the next day and bring back the pack-horse to Deep Creek. Worried that he couldn't find them when he arrived in Nelson, he informed the police, who sent out a search party.

Suspicions of foul play were soon aroused, and the finger was pointed at the four strangers who stayed at Jervis's store in Canvastown.

As the search for the Deep Creek party escalated, a reward and a pardon was offered and a town crier called for volunteers to help. Among the first to enlist was Theopolis Mabille — an engineer who had surveyed the building of the track. He was also an accomplished artist, and his sketches of the search itself and the bodies of the victims, along with his fanciful ones depicting the killings, later did much to arouse the public's indignation.

The search soon became the main topic of conversation in Nelson and nearby districts. Eventually over 100 men were searching the Maungatapu Track, but in vain. They didn't have long to wait, however. The police soon realised that the strangers who had stayed in Jervis's hut were probably the same four men who had been splashing their money around Nelson. They also fitted the descriptions of four men suspected of robbery and murder on the West Coast goldfields, and who were wanted in connection with the murder of a surveyor named Dobson.

The four men were soon arrested, but admitted nothing, although they made no attempt to account for the large amount of money found with them. Then the missing men's horse was found, shot through the head. But as long as there were no bodies, and Burgess and his men stayed quiet, they were safe.

MARLBOROUGH HISTORICAL SOCIETY ARCHIVES

The police separated Levy, hoping that he would cave in more readily than the others. But it was Sullivan who took fright and confessed, turning Queen's evidence in exchange for a pardon — and also claiming various rewards totalling 1000 pounds. He confessed to being an accomplice in the murders, but denied taking part in any of the killings himself. He said that he kept guard on the road while the others took the men away and killed them. He also fingered Burgess and Levy for the death of Jamie Battle, and blamed Burgess and Kelly for George Dobson's murder.

He also told the searchers where the bodies were, and the dead men were found on 30 June 1866. They were brought back to Nelson and laid out before a horrified public. Thousands of people came to see the bodies before burial, and a huge crowd followed the procession to the cemetery; it was Nelson's largest funeral ever. Jamie Battle's body was also soon found in the spot described by Sullivan, and he was laid to rest along with the four other victims.

Attention was then focused on the alleged killers, and the trial attracted so much interest that it had to be shifted from the courthouse to the larger provincial hall. All the gang save Sullivan were charged with the murders of the four Maungatapu victims, as well as Jamie Battle. Kelly and Levy pleaded not guilty, but Burgess stunned the court with a confession written in his cell, which he proceeded to read out for five hours. The confession began with a long semi-religious ramble to demonstrate his new-found piety, and fully admitted his part in several murders. But it was also full of vindictiveness and hate towards Sullivan. According to Burgess, he and Sullivan had done all the killings, and Kelly and Levy were innocent of any of the murders. They, not Sullivan, had been lookouts on occasion, but had not even known about the Maungatapu murders until well after the event, as they had gone on ahead while he and Sullivan killed the four men.

Burgess said that he and Sullivan had killed Battle, and that Sullivan had described in great detail how he and another man had killed George Dobson.

During the following trial, Levy was the only one represented by a lawyer; the two others defended themselves. So the public were treated to the spectacle of Burgess and Kelly rigorously cross-examining Sullivan in the witness box. At the end of the trial, Kelly collapsed with hysterical exhaustion and had to be given a chair. But Burgess was icy cool. "I stand before you as an actual murderer," he told the jury in his summing up.

In getting back at Sullivan, Burgess had signed his own death warrant. But the jury did not believe that Kelly and Levy were mere spectators, and took just 55 minutes to find all three men guilty of murder. They were immediately sentenced to death.

During the trial, Burgess had hammered away at the fact that Sullivan had helped him kill Battle, knowing that he had no immunity from prosecution for this murder. "He is the actual murderer, along with myself," he declared. The authorities were quite prepared to believe Burgess on this one, and the very next day, Sullivan was tried for the murder of Battle. The jury took just 25 minutes to find him guilty and he was sentenced to death. He collapsed in the dock, but luckily for him, his sentence was later commuted to life imprisonment.

The rest of the gang were not so lucky, and a hanging was set for 5 October 1866. Burgess whiled away his time by writing his memoirs, an astonishing expanded version of his courtroom confession that detailed his entire life of crime. Burgess makes no bones about the fact that he chose a life of crime as a lad in London, but also says that he was brutalised from an early age — first by his foster family and later when he was imprisoned in the notorious hulks of Victoria, Australia — prison ships where Burgess was continually flogged and kept in solitary confinement.

Burgess hoped that his memoirs would be published, and that the money would go to his girlfriend, Carrie, to support their unborn child. I was unable to find out if Carrie ever got a penny from their sale. But I did discover that, after several years of being suppressed by the government, *The Confessions of Richard Burgess* were published in 1886, by one Alfred Hibble, who at the time of the trial was editor of the *Nelson Examiner* and visited Burgess frequently in his cell.

In fact, Burgess became something of a celebrity for the brief remainder of his life. Everyone wanted a piece of the action. Clergymen were calling constantly, and practically dictating the more religious bits of his confession, some had alleged. Also hanging around were two travelling phrenologists who were most anxious to examine the killers' heads after the executions. Phrenology was the pseudo-science of reading a person's personality by feeling the bumps on their head, and was all the rage.

On the morning of the hanging, the newspapers reported that Burgess seemed happy and excited, chatting with those present, and said, although it was the day of his death, "I consider it the morning of my wedding." He formally repeated his assertions for the last time that his fellow prisoners were innocent of any crime, and called on God to receive his soul.

Burgess mounted the scaffold calmly before kissing the noose and saying, "I greet you as a prelude to Heaven."

*T*he death masks of (from left) Burgess, Kelly and Levy. D. MARTEN, GREENSTONE PICTURES

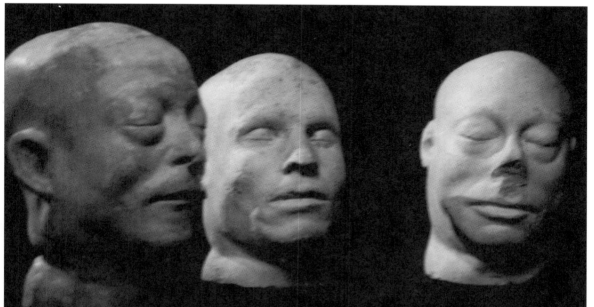

Although declaring his innocence, Levy seemed resigned to his fate, but Kelly was not so happy. He read out a long statement claiming his innocence, but went on so long that the sheriff told him to shut up. Kelly was dragged screaming up the steps of the scaffold, and even on the trapdoor, he was yelling, "Don't be in a hurry." Burgess apparently told him to "Shut up and die like a man."

After the trapdoor swung open, Kelly still refused to succumb — he jerked and thrashed on the end of the rope, and the hangman had to swing on his legs three times to finish him off. Outside the gaol, the crowd cheered as the black flag flew.

Later that day, the killers' heads were decapitated by two doctors present, and the plaster death masks now held by the Nelson Museum were made. Some say that this was done on the orders of the phrenologists, who were supported by the local governor, himself a noted phrenologist.

The memorial erected in memory of Jamie Battle and other victims of the Burgess gang. D. MARTEN, GREENSTONE PICTURES

So ended one of the bloodiest chapters in New Zealand criminal history. Local legend has it that the murderers were buried in the prison yard, and many years later, when a school was built on the site, the bones were dug up and kept in a box for many years by one of the schoolteachers. The killers were eventually reinterred just outside the cemetery gates in an unmarked grave. Inside the graveyard are their victims. The citizens of Nelson obviously felt that they should not be forgotten and erected a fine monument over their grave. There was apparently much argument about what the inscription should be, but finally, it was decided; "Vengeance is mine — I will repay, saith the Lord."

But vengeance did not extend to turncoat Joseph Sullivan. After eight years in prison, he was pardoned by the Governor of New Zealand and put on a ship to England. He later turned up in Melbourne, where he tried to rejoin his wife and children. But he was recognised by the police, and forced to leave town.

No one knows what happened to him next, but an Auckland newspaper in 1911 reported that a man who had just died in a local boarding-house was believed by many to have been Joseph Sullivan — the last of the Maungatapu Murderers. If so, he would by this stage have been well over 100 years old, but who knows? Stranger things have happened.

Over Niagara Falls

A TOMB WITH A view: from the Manukau Heads on Auckland's west coast, the vista stretches around to where the Southern Motorway slithers out of sight to the south. It's impressive and it's what Bobby Leach would see if he could sit on the edge of his own grave. He would appreciate it, too, as he had a head for heights — he went over the Niagara Falls in a barrel. This I found out because it is written on his gravestone, which nestles into a steep hillside in Auckland's Hillsborough Cemetery. The full inscription reads:

IN LOVING MEMORY
OF BOBBY LEACH
WORLD FAMOUS BY HIS TRIP OVER
NIAGARA FALLS IN A BARREL.
DIED 28TH APRIL 1926
AGED 69 YEARS

World famous! I'd never even heard of him. Why wasn't this intrepid Kiwi known to me? In New Zealand we are usually very quick to turn anyone who does something the least bit interesting into a national hero, especially if it's some kind of physical feat. So my next search began.

I found an answer to my queries in a substantial obituary to Bobby in the *Auckland Herald* the day after he died, Thursday 29th April 1926:

EPITAPH

BOBBY LEACH DEAD

NIAGARA FALLS EXPLOIT

DEATH FOLLOWS ACCIDENT

RECENT FALL ON THE STREET

Bobby Leach, known to the world as the only man to survive the feat of going over Niagara Falls in a barrel, died in a private hospital in Auckland yesterday. He was aged 69 years.

After a life of intrepid exploits and hairbreadth escapes, the actual incident that led to his death seems like one of those ironies of fate that bestrew the pages of ancient fiction, for having defied death a hundred times he at last owed his end to a piece of orange peel. Mr Leach had just concluded a lecturing tour in New Zealand and was strolling along the pavement close to his flat in Princes Street when he slipped on the orange peel and broke his leg. That was on February 26, since when he had been an invalid.

There can be little doubt that the leg injuries he received during his memorable drift in the barrel were responsible for the weakening of the limb that was broken. Complications set in and on Monday the leg was amputated, but the patient rapidly weakened and died.

Mr Leach was born in Lancaster, England and went to America when 18 years of age. He was then an expert swimmer and began his career by giving exhibitions of trick swimming and diving. He served for three seasons with Barnum and Bailey's celebrated circus, performing high diving feats. In 1908 he dived from the Steel Arch Bridge at Niagara, a height of 208 feet, said to be the highest dive in the world. He crossed the dangerous Whirlpool Rapids at Niagara in a barrel no fewer than four times and on July 25, 1911, he performed the exploit for which he has been world famous, descending the river in a steel barrel for two and a half miles and eventually dropping over the Horseshoe Fall, a height of 163 feet. The shock broke the harness by which he was secured and his jaw and both kneecaps were broken.

Early in his life Mr Leach was interested in aeronautics and before the day of the aeroplane performed sensational parachute descents from balloons, in one case dropping a distance of over two miles. When the aeroplane supplanted the balloon he performed the feat of dropping from one racing aeroplane to another by means of a rope ladder. In fact he accomplished this risky exploit at Lake Erie only three years ago, when 67 years of age.

In the course of his lecture tours, Mr Leach visited Great Britain, Canada and Australia. He was a keen billiard player and a winner of several championship matches in the United States.

His wife and daughter, who accompanied him to New Zealand, remain at their flat in Princes Street.

The internment will take place at Hillsborough Cemetery tomorrow afternoon.

To appease his disappointed public, Bobby navigated the Whirlpool Rapids in a barrel for a third time, and then three months later announced he would make another attempt at the falls. This time he would use a specially designed lifeboat. It was about 20 feet long, cigar-shaped and entirely closed in. The interior was lined with rubber to stop the occupant being bruised when tossed about. Bobby's reputation was on the line and a fellow stunter, "Red" Hill, had threatened to go over in a load of hay if Bobby chickened out.

Fortunately for Bobby, he had the sense to test the lifeboat first. Along with his wife Sadie, who was there to make sure Bobby didn't jump in at the last minute, he watched the boat plunge over the brink and reappear five minutes later as "a small heap of wreckage floating around in the foam and spume at the foot of the falls".

It was back to the drawing board, and Bobby constructed another steel barrel, which in June 1911 he used to go down the Whirlpool Rapids for a fourth time. Yet again he announced to the world that he was about to take on the mighty falls, this time in the same design of steel barrel that had served him so well through the rapids.

It should be noted at this point that although no man had ever been over the falls and lived to tell the tale, they had in fact been conquered. By a woman. In October 1901, Annie Edson Taylor made her trip over the mighty cataract in a crude wooden cask. She was a large woman and had great difficulty getting in. This alone took over an hour. Fifty-five minutes later, having passed over the brink, she was brought to the shore where, because of her great weight and helplessness, she had to be cut out with a saw. Incredibly, she suffered little injury.

Nearly 12years later on 25 July 1911, as Bobby prepared to climb into his steel barrel for his long awaited attempt, Annie Taylor had this to say: "I don't think he will make the trip. I have no faith in Leach or his assertions. He is a man in whom I have never placed any dependence. Still, I wish him well and have no hard feelings for him in any way. I would be the first to congratulate him if he came out sucessfully, but he will never do it."

Well, Bobby did do it, and I give you a blow-by-blow account of his trip as described by the *Buffalo Express*:

OVER FALLS IN A BARREL

Bobby Leach made the perilous trip and isn't very much the worse for it.

WELL SHAKEN UP
NOT ANXIOUS TO REPEAT

With Mrs Taylor who did the same feat in 1901 he exclaims, "Never again."

Bobby Leach of Niagara Falls, this afternoon went over the Horseshoe Falls in a barrel and still lives. He was battered, but his injuries were superficial, and, it is believed will not prove serious.

Watched by the police on both sides of the river and rebuffed by the wind, Leach was forced yesterday to abandon his trip. Today conditions were more favourable. The wind was less severe and he moved up the river to La Salle out of reach of the local police, but the river was too rough and he had to defer the start to this afternoon.

About 1.30 o'clock, Leach with moving picture operators boarded a launch and with the red steel barrel in tow, started out into the river. The boat had a hard time making headway in the heavy seas, but made Navy Island, about a mile above the brink in safety.

There everything was made shipshape. Bobby wearing his shore clothes, entered the barrel, while the picture men busied themselves. He was strapped in a hammock that was slung lengthwise of the barrel, a canvas contrivance reinforced with bands of leather. When the head of the barrel was screwed down, Leach gave the boatmen the word and they started away from Navy Island for the middle of the Canadian channel. It was 2.56 o'clock when Leach started for the cataract.

As soon as the barrel was caught in the break of the upper rapids, it sped swiftly towards the brink. Over the rocks it dashed in the onrush of the current, bobbing and dancing over the waves, the red hull always in view of the thousands that lined the bank from Chippawa to the brink. And in that section of water Leach suffered the most. For much of the time the barrel was crosswise of the stream. About 100 feet from the brink the barrel swung about and the end smashed against a huge rock, partly submerged. A large section of the end of laminated wood was knocked off.

It was exactly 3.13 o'clock when the barrel plunged into the abyss, a drop of 158 feet. Less than a minute elapsed until it was seen again tossing in the spume of the cataract. The river was so high that it was swiftly borne out from the fall into the stream and close to the Canadian shore. The angry river shook it and tumbled it terribly but always the barrel moved onward until it reached a point where it reached an eddy and twirled like a top. Frank Bender of Chippawa, when he saw the state of affairs, took off his clothes, grasped a rope and swam out to the barrel, attaching the rope to one of the handles.

The barrel was dragged up to the rocks and a dozen men rushed up and began to work frantically to release the head of the barrel. They heard rappings from within and knew that Leach was still alive.

Still in his barrel, the cover off, Bobby calmly observed:

"Well, they ain't got nothin on me."

For he had been heckled much of late that he had talked of making the falls trip for the last eight years, when an old woman had done it almost on the spur of the moment.

But Leach was a sorry sight when he was taken from the barrel. He was bleeding from the right ear and was utterly exhausted. Yet as he stood in his barrel he waved his hands to the crowd that lined the banks. Leach was carried over the rocks to the power station. He thought his leg was broken. When a doctor arrived Bobby was almost in a state of collapse and oxygen was administered. An examination showed Leach had a badly sprained right knee, a contusion of the head and a black eye. He was put in a carriage and brought to the top of the bank. His teeth chattering from the wet and the cold, he was received by the crowd and the moving picture men before being driven home to his little restaurant and put to bed.

"The rapids were worse than the big drop," said Leach. "The tumbling I got above the falls were like to kill me. Course there was a bit of a jar when I landed at the bottom, but it was up river that I felt the trip the worst." Asked if he would make the trip again, he said,

"Not on your bloomin life. Once is enough for Bobby. But they ain't got nothin on me now."

BOBBY LEACH'S Awful Plunge over Niagara Falls, July 25th, 1911.
(Copyright 1911, by Photo Specialty Co.)

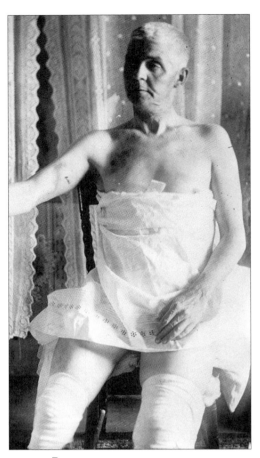

Leach sustained serious injuries during his triumphant trip over the falls.
COURTESY NIAGARA FALLS LIBRARY

So, AT AGE 54, Bobby Leach became headline news around the world, and unlike Annie Edson Taylor who died a pauper in a poorhouse, he was to make the most of his success. Using the film he had made of his death-defying plunge, he toured the vaudeville circuits of the world up until the time of his death in 1926.

Not that he rested on his laurels where stunts were concerned. Even in the year before his death, at age 68, he attempted to swim the Niagara River below the falls. He was halfway across when, gasping for breath, he lost his false teeth, which caused him to founder and signal for the rowing boat to pick him up. In March of that same year, he was threatening to go over the falls again in "a new sort of craft, different from anything that had been offered for his use before". However, the trip did not materialise and his backers were disappointed with the "faithless promises made by the little navigator". In October 1925, a week before Bobby and his family were to leave on his fateful tour to Australia and New Zealand, he promised to make one last appearance that would be a "real thriller". He would parachute from high above the falls wearing an inflated inner tube. Much was made in the press of this upcoming stunt, but nowhere could I find a report of it actually taking place. I suspect that like his bid to conquer the falls for a second time, it came to nothing. At this time, Bobby was described as "the veteran performer through whose bones the fever of unrest was again beginning to creep". I get the feeling, though, that what Bobby imagined he was still capable of doing and what in reality he was capable of doing were two different things. Certainly, he was often accused of making false promises, and one newspaper cynically wondered if they were merely to "attract tourists to his place of business in Youngstown".

While Bobby may have felt the "fever of unrest" creeping through his bones, what he didn't know was that cancer was creeping through his bones as well. On his death certificate, it gives the cause of death as sarcoma of the femur. Bobby had bone cancer. Even if he had survived the amputation of his leg following his slip on the orange peel, Bobby's days were numbered. After his death, his wife Sadie stayed on in Auckland for several months before returning to Buffalo, where she lived out the rest of her life.

She died in 1942, aged 66. Two years earlier, she had given an interview to the local paper: "It's all so long ago. We went to so many places and met so many people, but our generation is forgotten now." She had met Bobby when he parachuted by mistake into her parents' back garden, ruining a rose bush. Struck by her beauty, Bobby saw to it that all his descents were made in the vicinity of her house until he had won her. "He would stick to one thing for a while, then he would be off on some new plan, and we would travel for a few months, with a circus or carnival or, in later years, on vaudeville tours with the lectures and moving pictures."

Bobby had certainly made the most out of the film of his falls ride. For 15 years he flogged it around the world, taking it through the United States, Canada, Britain, Europe, South Africa, Australia and New Zealand. In fact, Bobby showed his film so much that he wore it out. Always the astute businessman, he had another made, but this time the barrel went over without him inside.

I would love to see that piece of film but I doubt if it still exists. I've had no luck tracking it down, nor have I traced any of Bobby's descendants. Sadie's death notice said she was survived only by a son-in-law, so sadly she must have outlived her own daughter Pearl. Coincidently, it was in Pearl Street that Sadie would die.

Over Niagara Falls In A Barrel

A. SCRANTON presents

Bobby Leach

The Only Man in the World who has performed this feat

COURTESY NIAGARA FALLS LIBRARY

As for Bobby, I salute him. Many people said many things about Bobby Leach, and although he will go down in history as the man who survived Niagara Falls only to come to grief on an orange peel, these comments remain as a testimony to his pluck and character:

"Bobby, you are the gamest man in the world." — Duke of Connaught
"All nations should be proud of such a man as Bobby Leach." — William Taft, President of the United States of America.
"A small man with a big amount of nerve and pluck." — *Toronto Globe*
"The Press looks upon Bobby Leach's feats as one of the world's greatest achievements." — *New York Journal*
"Champion of all champions, Bobby Leach." — *New York Herald*

Towards the end of his life, he may have cut something of a sad figure desperately trying to recapture the glory of earlier days, but there is no doubt that he lived life to the full and without regret. As Sadie put it, "He was never sorry about anything he did. That was his business, and he either had a lot of nerve or no nerve, I don't know which."

Chinese Coffins

SOMEWHERE IN A REMOTE village of rural China, there once stood a shrine inscribed with these words:

LET THE SCATTERED FLOCK RETURN

It was noted in the diary of a Presbyterian minister visiting China last century. It's gone now, the forces of Communism having reduced to rubble many shrines and sacred places.

To me, this lost monument has become the most poignant epitaph of the Chinese who flocked to the South Island goldfields in the 1860s. Many, of course, were never to return. They died here, forever foreigners in an alien soil, their gravestones slim tablets of stone in forgotten corners of Christian cemeteries — or in some cases in watery graves. But I'll get to that.

It was to the "New Gold Hill", the brown hills and turbulent rivers of Central Otago, that hundreds of Chinese were sent by their villages to find gold — and return home. Many of the early books about the Central Otago goldfields give romantic accounts of the brave pioneers who struck out to the colonies to start a new life. But the Chinese were always different: they were not colonists; they never intended to settle here; they often worked the tailings left by the Europeans. They were hated for their strange ways, their frugality, their gambling and opium, and mostly for their success.

Many did not travel directly from mainland China. Some journeyed via the Victorian goldfields in Australia. At first, they were encouraged to come here to provide a cheap labour force. However, the tide turned when Richard John Seddon came into power and passed a bill in 1896 to limit their immigration because he did not feel they were a "desirable sort of colonist". Chinese workers were made to pay poll tax on entry to New Zealand. Here again I was encountering intolerance shown by Anglo-Saxon settlers to cultures different from their own.

A Chinese gravestone in Cromwell Cemetery — one immigrant who did not return.

One of the most bizarre stories of the early Chinese immigrants, and one that was to provoke my next search, involved their dead. Cheong Shing Tong was a burial society responsible for the exhumation of hundreds of Chinese graves between 1883 and 1902. Why? To fulfil the Chinese belief that their bones must be returned to the land of their birth to ensure that their descendants can perform the ancestral rites of worship.

To the Chinese, many of them Buddhists and Confucianists, getting buried in their own soil was part of their journey to Eternal Life. To have your family make offerings at your grave or shrine kept your spirit alive and meant the gods would look favourably upon your descendants when they, in turn, died. The fact that so many were buried in New Zealand because they were too poor to return, had grown old or met with tragic accidents here must have been abhorrent to them. This soon became apparent to the prominent prosperous Chinese in New Zealand, so they began a society, paid for by subscription, to guarantee members passage back to China — dead or alive.

Roughly translated, Cheong Shing Tong means "Splendid Goodness Society". Their main role was to exhume graves (some were years old), clean the bones, wrap them in calico, place them in specially prepared lead-lined coffins, and pay for their shipment back to China.

Of course, this all sounded grisly and pagan to the Europeans. "So much expense and trouble," I could almost hear the canny colonials sniff. When the first exhumation took place just before 1883, there was public outcry because it was regarded as desecration and there were fears that opening graves would bring disease and contaminate the water supply. The Health Department became involved, and the exhumations were performed under their strictest supervision, although the burial society continued to provide their own staff to clean the bones. They were reported as being quite nonchalant about their strange task, "eating lunch at the gravesite calmly without washing their hands", though this could well have been propaganda as anti-Chinese feeling was running high at that time.

In fact, a law was instigated to discourage Chinese immigration by prohibiting the exhumation of their graves. It is possible the Chinese got wise to this because, in later years, they buried their dead in lead-lined coffins for easy dispatch. But older graves still had to be exhumed in the same way as the first with the same meticulous care, every single bone cleaned and wrapped.

My interest lay with the last, and what was to be the fateful, shipment of 1902. This was the largest made and many of the coffins to be sent had been stored at a warehouse in Kaikorai Valley near Dunedin before being loaded onto the *Ventnor* for the journey. A further consignment was loaded in Wellington; so in all 499 Chinese souls were to return home. But it was not to be. The *Ventnor* sank off the Hokianga on 28 October 1902.

Imagine the grief of the Chinese community, because to them a body lost in water is irretrievable, the spirit cast into limbo. Choie Kum Poy, the son of prominent Dunedin businessman Choie (Charlie) Sew Hoy was reported as saying that his father had died a second time when his coffin sank with the ship.

What did I know at this point? The books and press clippings I'd read were conflicting as to the number of Chinese coffins aboard the *Ventnor* but unanimous that the entire "strange cargo", including several hundred tonnes of Greymouth coal and a tonne of the Chinese fungus muk yee, had sunk with the ship, never to be seen again.

I was re-reading a chapter of Dr James Ng's book *Windows on a Chinese Past* when a sentence jumped out at me: "... ten coffins floated ashore . . . .". I was astounded! The source of Dr Ng's reference was the diary of a Presbyterian minister of the time, Revd Alexander Don, who had been heavily involved with

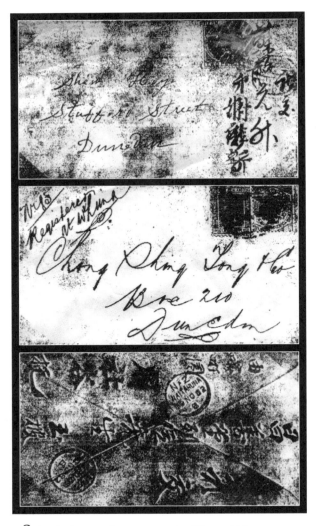

Subscription envelopes sent to the Cheong Shing Tong Society. COURTESY G. FRANCIS

the Chinese since the goldfield days. How did he know that any coffins had washed ashore? Why had I never found any other reference to this? I wanted to see those diaries for myself.

However, the doors of the Knox Presbyterian College Library in Dunedin were firmly bolted against me. The diaries are stored there but I was declined permission to see them because of their fragility. There are no other copies. Why? Well, it could come down to Ṙevd Don's relationship with the Chinese. According to Ng (and I had also heard this elsewhere), Don held the Chinese in contempt. His mission was to convert them from their heathen ways, and presumably his jottings are so offensive that it is deemed best to keep them locked away. I didn't want to dismiss the Revd Don altogether, though; after all he was a product of his times, and something told me that, despite his purported views, he did have a lot of contact with the Chinese, so if I read more about him I'd find out more about those coffins.

Don's Chinese flock was scattered around the goldfields like elusive nuggets. His accounts of trekking on foot into Central Otago to visit them are recorded in his most famous published work: *Inland Tours*. But it is the extracts from Don's personal diaries recorded in Dr Ng's book that give many fascinating insights into the beliefs of the Chinese. That's where the prominent Dunedin Chinese businessman Charlie Sew Hoy comes into the story.

Despite Don's best efforts, very few Chinese dropped their "heathen ways" to enter the Christian fold, and Charlie Sew Hoy was no exception. I could surmise that this was maddening to Revd Don because Sew Hoy had more influence over his countrymen than anyone else. He was originally from the district of China once called Upper Panyu, a big success in Otago. He shaped the developments of goldmining, especially dredging on the Shotover River near Queenstown. When the gold business dried up, Sew Hoy moved to Dunedin and, by 1871, established a merchant business with a fellow countryman called Chew Chong of Taranaki in the export to China of the muk yee fungus, of which a shipment was on board the *Ventnor* when it sank. Both men are remembered as pillars of the community. The name Sew Hoy is still well known in Dunedin today.

While his friend Chew Chong embraced European society, Sew Hoy kept a low profile, especially in the face of increasing hostilities towards the Chinese, worked toward the benefit of his own people, and remained most definitely Chinese. It is said he held a high office in the Cheong Shing Tong, the burial society, and held meetings at his own premises in Dunedin. In 1901, in the year before the 1902 shipment, Charlie Sew Hoy died. As a distinguished man, he had a fine rimu coffin instead of the plain varnished kauri of his compatriots.

Nine old men were to accompany the dead home to their final resting place, but this was not to be, as the *Auckland Weekly News* of 7 April 1904 relates:

> . . . The last voyage of the ill-fated steamer *Ventnor*, in 1902, carrying a celestial cargo of the mortal remains of some 500 Chinese, constitutes one of the strangest pages in New Zealand's history . . .

The ship, hopelessly off course, struck a reef near the coast of Opunake, and while attempts were made to bail water, the ship's pumps were not equal to the task. The captain, who drowned trying to escape the ship, was found negligent. Built in Glasgow by a reputable shipping company, the *Ventnor* was originally a collier, built to take coal to the British Naval Station on the China Sea. Mariners are a superstitious lot, and it seems the *Ventnor* was considered a "hoodoo" ship because she had already run aground on her maiden voyage, a short time before.

I scanned Ng's book and Don's published works to find other references to the sinking. Revd Don provided an intriguing twist: he recorded strange rumours circulating amongst the Chinese community about the sinking. As I said, to the Chinese, those who went down with the *Ventnor* died a second time, but some asked why, if the spirits of the dead had "ling" (spiritual energy), could 500 of them not have saved themselves and the ship?

An explanation was apparently readily to hand: the ghosts themselves caused the

Flashback of exhumation scene. PHOTO: SIMION YOUNG

Chinese miners from last century. HOCKEN LIBRARY E2448/5

vessel to founder. Though he didn't come right out and say it, Revd Don implied that a past conflict between Sew Hoy and another Chinese businessman, Kong Cheung Ling, whose body was also aboard, was the cause of spiritual ructions. Sew Hoy was supposed to have defamed Kong for misappropriating burial society funds 20 years previously when Kong had been the treasurer. Don intimated that because Sew Hoy was respected, influential and wealthy, his accusation against the poorer man was upheld. But all's fair in the spirit world, and some believed their spirits were fighting it out. Writes Don:

> . . . The fight spread to their clansmen and partisans till nearly all aboard were involved in a fearful conflict. Several of the living passengers reported hideous sounds and awesome convulsions in the air . . .

There were also suggestions of yet more ghostly strife between two other dead men on board, one having robbed the other back in China. The other (some said) had got his revenge by poisoning his countryman.

The idea of spiritual forces slugging it out is fascinating, but the cynic in me wondered whether the stories were manipulated, perhaps even by Don as revenge on Sew Hoy for his aloofness to Christianity or as a threat to those remaining who did not embrace his teachings.

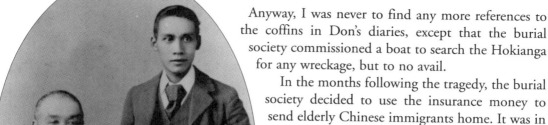

Sew Hoy and his son.

Anyway, I was never to find any more references to the coffins in Don's diaries, except that the burial society commissioned a boat to search the Hokianga for any wreckage, but to no avail.

In the months following the tragedy, the burial society decided to use the insurance money to send elderly Chinese immigrants home. It was in those black days afterwards that the society faded in importance and soon died out. The story died, too, though from bits and pieces I gleaned from the press, I discovered that two lifeboats were found at Omapere and the captain's boat further north. Nothing more. The whole incident was overshadowed by Seddon's diplomatic visit to Britain and the sinking of the *Elingamite* off Three Kings Island a few weeks later with a tragic loss of life.

So I closed the Otago chapter of the Chinese story and set my sights on the Hokianga. Who would know anything about 10 coffins floating ashore on a remote northern beach? After much thought, I tried the Dargaville Maritime Museum. Bingo! The staff put me in touch with the curator Noel Hilliam, an amateur archaeologist who specialises in shipwrecks. Noel even knows the exact spot where the *Ventnor* lies, 26 km off the Hokianga heads. He told me that 10 of the coffins had washed up at Kawerua, South Hokianga. So, if their resting place was not the sea, where were they buried?

The place is called Chinaman's Hill. A fenced grassy knoll, just up from the beach, in a remote part of the Waipoua Forest. It's not widely known or surveyed, nor are the graves marked.

Why? It's down to old sailor's folklore really. Those old salts, who had mostly jumped ship and chose to hide in the remote hills, strongly believed that the Chinese were buried with their gold. They encouraged mystique about the setting, not just as a result of their own superstitions about disturbing the dead but because they feared desecration of the graves because of the gold.

This was stirring stuff. I asked Noel if I could visit the site. There are two ways you can go: through the rugged Waipoua Forest from the Dargaville end; or a day's walk along the beach from Dargaville until you reach Kawerua — not exactly a day jaunt from Auckland in sensible shoes. And there was another reason why I couldn't just drop by for a visit: Chinaman's Hill is part of an ancestral burial ground. It is tapu.

The Maori have buried their dead in caves below the site for centuries. The future of Waipoua Forest depends on Treaty of Waitangi tribunal claims, but it seems the Department of Conservation and the local iwi have a good relationship in terms of protecting the site from marauding tourists — and TV crews! The Maori of the area feel strongly about respecting the dead. They treat the Chinese buried there as they treat their own, with dignity and distance. And, in the Maori tradition, they have never marked the graves.

The story had taken on a cross-cultural turn — Chinese buried on Maori land, entwining the two peoples forever. But who buried them? Why were they buried in an ancestral Maori burial ground? Would tapu have been broken in the act? Why not an ordinary cemetery or a plot up from the beach? Why did the Chinese not reclaim the bodies and send them on to China? Or were they never informed? We may never know.

I walked along a lonely stretch of beach as I pondered these questions, idly tossing the occasional pebble into the sea. It suddenly struck me — those coffins were supposed to have been lead-lined, made specially by a Greymouth leadsmith. Why then did they not sink? How come they floated ashore?

The answer was in Dr Ng's book. The 10 coffins did not belong to the burial society, but were loaded on to the *Ventnor* at Wellington, paid for by individuals of Zengcheng origin. Those that suggested the spirits were quarrelling aboard the ship might have concluded that as the Zengcheng dead were from Wellington, it is likely they were far removed from the feuding between the other Chinese from Dunedin. Perhaps what saved these coffins from a watery grave was their being free from the spiritual strife going

The Ventnor *sinking off the Hokianga.* AUCKLAND WEEKLY NEWS, 13 NOV. 1902, COURTESY NZ HERALD

on between the dead . . . A more likely explanation, however, is that the Zengcheng coffins would not have been made in Greymouth, so may not have been lead-lined and were possibly held in a hold just below deck. The bulk of the shipment — deceased natives of the Upper Panyu and Hua districts — were stored below in the mortuary, attended by elderly Chinese "bodyguards". I'm surmising that when the ship broke up and began to sink, the 10 coffins broke free from the wreck, and because they were not lead-lined, floated ashore at Kawerua.

This made me think of the New Zealand film about the Chinese in Central Otago, *Illustrious Energy*, directed by Leon Narbey. Two miners dig up the bones of a family member who had obviously died many years before. They clean, wrap and place the bones in an ornate box, no larger than a grocery carton. Could this have been the case with the Zengcheng coffins? Were they smaller and lighter?

One thing that clinched this theory was my discovery that a further two coffins had washed up at Mitimiti, north Hokianga, at about the same time. I should probably point out that no one knows for sure that there are exactly 10 coffins buried at Chinaman's Hill. Revd Don does say 10 in his diaries, but he could have meant that a total of 10 had survived the wreck, not being specific about where they washed up.

There is a real story attached to the Mitimiti coffins and I could surmise that a similar event happened when the coffins were discovered at Kawerua. Two Maori men were fishing one morning when they discovered two "boxes" on the beach. Being isolated and not knowing anything about the wreck of the *Ventnor*, curiosity got the better of them and they opened the boxes.

To their horror, they discovered bones. Not wanting to put a tapu on the beach (because that's what happens even today when a dead body is found) or to be reprimanded by their people, the two men carried the coffins to a remote cave, also a tapu site.

However, they were caught hiding the bodies in the cave, so it was decided to seal the entrance and discourage anyone from ever breaking tapu. This story passed into local legend.

There is also a story that another two coffins were found and sent to Rawene for shipment to China, but I've never found anything to substantiate the rumour. Perhaps the real reason that none of the others were claimed was because they were simply not insured. And, of course, the Hokianga was, and still is, an extremely remote spot, its coastline an infamous ships' graveyard.

So what have we now? Some coffins, a ship, spiritual foul play, negligence and tragedy. Is this the end of the story? No one visits these lonely spots with offerings of food and drink. No one sits by the graves to address their spirits. No headstones even mark their resting place. It all happened so long ago, but the lost souls have not been forgotten.

Duncan Sew Hoy, great-grandson of Charlie Sew Hoy, has a dream, in fact, a burning ambition, to raise finance (probably over a million dollars) to locate the *Ventnor*, lift out the coffins and send them to their destination: the yellow earth of China.

ove Letter

DRIVING DOWN INTO TRAVELLERS Valley, in the high country south of Nelson, I felt as though I were making a pilgrimage. A number of people connected in some way to the Augarde family had come this way before me, and all as part of, or in memorial to, the tragedies that have added renown to the Augarde family history. Rising at the head of the valley is Mt Augarde, its name standing as testimony to the esteem in which this family was and is held. A monument to a tragic episode in the family's history lies in the mountain's shadow; a lonely grave which reads:

IN MEMORY OF
IVANHOE STANLEY AUGARDE
BORN SURREY ENGLAND 1844
DIED NEAR THIS SPOT
29 JANUARY 1868

This stone was set here in the 1970s, when four men came up by Land-Rover to see this landscape for themselves and to lay this memorial stone to their ancestor, Ivanhoe.

It is an unlikely setting for a tragic love story, but that is what happened here and why Ivanhoe Augarde lies buried in such a desolate spot. At 1200 metres above sea level, the winters are bitter and long and the summers short. It is isolated, very isolated. As far as the eye can see, this land is a sheep and cattle station. A station hut near Ivanhoe's grave provides the only shelter out here now. Few of the early farm buildings or accommodation houses have survived.

It's a place you actually have to see before you can fully understand how a landscape can send people slightly mad. The day I chose to visit this desolate spot was one of those magically clear, crisp South Island days that can make you forget you ever had a sinus problem. As our helicopter weaved its way up valley after valley there wasn't a cloud in the sky or a breath of wind, which was just as well because when we touched down and I set my foot on a ground that felt like concrete, it was still 5° below. For the entire day that we filmed there, I had to stand in the direct rays of the sun or else it was nigh on impossible to get my lips to speak to the camera. One day was enough for me. To be snowbound for months on end would definitely make you crazy.

I first read the story of Ivanhoe in a letter sent to me by family descendants, and I have been able to piece together added details of the story of Ivanhoe's death from newspaper reports and inquest evidence.

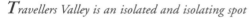

Travellers Valley is an isolated and isolating spot

Ivanhoe's father, Henry John Louis Augarde, was a stockbroker. Mid last century, there was a worldwide boom in the price of wool, and Henry Augarde would have seen the stocks rising and realised that there was a fortune to be made in the wool-rich colonies. So with his family, he migrated to New Zealand and settled in Nelson near the big sheep stations. His children would have been well educated but wholly unused to a pioneering life.

Nevertheless, by the time he was 23, Ivanhoe was managing a cattle station for a Mr Thomas Carter on the Clarence and Acheron Rivers near Carter's Accommodation House, where he stayed. He was engaged to Kate Gee, whose father ran the Rainbow Accommodation House up the Wairau Valley. Ivanhoe was obviously serious about marriage since he had bought a house and 10 acres of land. He visited Kate when he could, but the journey between Carter's and Rainbow House took four days. Correspondence would have been their easiest means of keeping in touch, and much of their romance was probably conducted by letter. Mail was distributed by travellers who followed red markers along the route directing them to the next house or station, which was the drop off and collection point. These red markers are a forerunner to the red post boxes that later covered the country.

Henry Augarde, Ivanhoe's father. AUCKLAND CITY LIBRARIES A13647

Then came the winter of 1867. It has gone down in New Zealand history as one of the most vicious winters ever. The snow came early and it didn't thaw until November. Every man, woman and child at every station was locked in by the elements and completely isolated.

According to those who still live around here, Ivanhoe and Kate had argued in the autumn and that winter kept them apart, without word to each other for months. Then spring came.

Here the story goes horribly wrong. It was some time close to Christmas 1867. Enter German Charlie, a stocky man, only about 5 foot 6 inches with a bushy red beard and a squint. From what I can glean reading the inquest testimonies, German Charlie was working for Ivanhoe at Carter's station, and apparently there was no love lost between them. Ivanhoe was very young to be a manager and perhaps Charlie resented that. Apart from this, the class system that lingered in the colonial psyche would have put Ivanhoe a step above his peers on the station. I can only imagine what those months of winter must have been like. My guide in the high country looked out across the valleys and said "It's the kind of country where people go mad."

With the better weather, German Charlie planned a trip down the valley, and Ivanhoe asked him to take a letter to Kate. Unfortunately, this provided German Charlie with an opportunity that would be the undoing of him and Ivanhoe. To spite his employer, Charlie showed the letter around every accommodation house and station he visited along the way. He handed it to shearers to read and made a great show of how much he was enjoying flaunting it at Ivanhoe's expense. Local legend has it that after

Acheron guesthouse still stands today

showing it round at Rainbow House where Kate lived, instead of passing it on to her he took it with him further north and pinned the letter to the mantelpiece at Top House.

When Ivanhoe heard what Charlie had done, he was angered beyond reason. There and then he went to find Charlie, determined to fight him. Later, Ivanhoe told his brother, Percy, about the fight saying Charlie wouldn't box English style, he wanted to fight "rough and tumble". The fight had to be stopped, and Ivanhoe had failed miserably in his attempt to get the better of Charlie.

Ivanhoe's father, Henry Augarde, was "accomplished at swordsmanship" and had even named his son after a swordsman of great repute. Had he instilled an outdated code of honour in Ivanhoe, a code of chivalry that was completely inappropriate in this new colony?

Ivanhoe hadn't seen his brother Percy for two years, but, soon after the fight, he wrote to ask him to come down to Carter's to join him. Percy arrived on 24 January and started work at the station immediately. By this time, German Charlie was labouring in the brickyard at Tarndale Station. Probably, after their fight, Ivanhoe had fired German Charlie and employed his brother in his place.

On Tuesday 28 January, Ivanhoe and Percy had dinner together with John Shaw (or Shou as it's printed in some papers) at Carter's Accommodation House at Acheron and then the brothers retired to their room there. Ivanhoe reappeared a short time later and asked for a pen. While his brother was asleep in bed, Ivanhoe sat up writing. On Wednesday, Ivanhoe left Carter's late in the morning while Percy was working in the stockyard. It wasn't until mid afternoon that Percy found the sheets of paper on top of his clean shirts and realised Ivanhoe had left a will and farewell letter to him. The letter read:

EPITAPH

Clarence Station
Jan 28 1868

Mr Percy Augarde

My Dear Brother, I bid you goodbye. We shall never meet again in this world. I am very sorry to leave you but it must be. I leave you all I have in the world; all is yours . . . You must go to Mr G Gee Wairau Valley and he will give you the deed of my land in Renwick Town and you must ask Miss Gee for a packet of letters I gave her to take care of for me. She has got the deeds to my land in the Wairau Valley . . . Now I must bid you goodbye and I hope you will get on better than your unhappy brother. We shall never meet in this world again my dear boy.

I.S. Augarde.

The letter contained some particulars about small amounts owing and some information about his horse, but it said nothing about what was going on in Ivanhoe's mind. According to Percy, Ivanhoe also wrote letters to Miss Gee and to his boss Thomas Carter and there was another letter for Percy which read more like a basic will. It outlined what Ivanhoe owned and who held the deeds to his properties and it finished with a simple "So goodbye dear brother."

That night at dinner, John Shaw thought Percy looked like he'd been crying. His eyes were bloodshot and he was very quiet, but when John pressed Percy for a reason he just said there was nothing wrong.

At about five o'clock, a stranger rode up to the Tarndale brick shed and asked one Charlie Sparrow to tell him who was at the station. Charlie, who had no idea who the man was, told him there was just himself and Charlie the German. Everyone else was down at the woolshed. German Charlie was working about 30 metres away but couldn't see who had approached the shed. Obviously not being one to chatter, Charlie Sparrow went straight back to his work. He heard the man call out "Charlie, I have a letter for you", then the sound of a gun being fired.

The stranger immediately spurred his horse to a gallop and took off up the valley. German Charlie lay dying. The bullet had caught him in the back and gone straight through him, exiting just below his heart. Charlie asked his mate who had shot him and the German replied "Ivy Augarde".

A couple of hours later, a man riding up the valley was nearing the junction of the Severn and Alma rivers when he found a horse, and not far from this he found the body of Ivanhoe Augarde. Ivanhoe was lying on his back, the butt of his rifle wedged against a cairn of stones and a gin bottle nearby. Ivanhoe had died from a gunshot wound to the head.

The next day, the man made it to Tarndale to report his find. Another rider took up the trail and headed off with the news to Carter's station. When Percy got the news, he rode out with two other men to Red Gate, the junction of the Alma and the Severn where Ivanhoe's body lay. When they got there, Percy was the only one to dismount and identify the body up close. The inquest report goes into some detail on the fatal injuries Ivanhoe had sustained. The musket with which Ivanhoe had shot himself was a very powerful weapon used for despatching cattle — it must have been a harrowing sight.

On the Friday following, a jury of 10 men and Ivanhoe's father rode out to the junction to see the body. When the jury were satisfied, Henry Augarde buried the body on higher ground and covered the grave with stones. This was the second son Henry had buried, another having drowned in the Motueka River. The cairn of stones was all that marked the grave until the memorial plaque was laid more than a hundred years later.

This must have been the end of a dream for Henry Augarde. He had brought his family out to a new settlement in a new country to try and break the land and make something for their future. It was the dream of a new life, of something better than England had held for them. In all, Henry had 18 children and lost most of them as well as his two wives. The epitaph on his second wife's grave in Nelson could well have been his own:

Where shall we find rest? Not here. The bruised heart shall find no rest from heaven apart.

Next to this grave is Henry's. He died penniless and is buried with no epitaph.

Of Kate Gee I know nothing more. Ivanhoe wrote a farewell letter to her the same night he wrote to his brother, but there's no indication of what was in either that letter or the letter that brought about this whole sad affair. Kate did not give evidence at the inquest and it seems the family moved away. I cannot imagine what all this tragedy must have been like for her. I wonder if Ivanhoe's actions appeared as extreme to her as they do to me. What could possibly have been in that letter that would drive a young man to murder and suicide?

German Charlie knew what was in that letter, but I'm sure he had no idea his heartless prank would ever lead to such reprisals. The site of Charlie's grave has been a matter of much speculation, but it seems an unmarked grave near Cat Creek, close to the site of the old Tarndale homestead, is likely to be the spot.

Initially, I felt desperate to know what was in that letter, but as time has gone on I have come to accept that it probably wouldn't have made sense of the tragedy anyway. Besides, the contents were only ever meant for Kate Gee, and it is perhaps right that they are secret from us.

affrey and Penn

GREAT BARRIER ISLAND IS one of those places that holds many stories and secrets, so I was not surprised when I stumbled across a lonely grave on a grassy slope overlooking Tryphena Harbour. The headstone is actually a piece of rock, with the following words carved by hand onto its face:

ROBERT
TAYLOR
MURDERED
19 JUNE 1886

There are no other graves here, it's not a cemetery, so it seemed likely that Taylor was murdered on this very spot or somewhere nearby. Scouting around, I could see what looked like the base of an old chimney, so I guessed there was a house here once. My map revealed that I was actually standing in Taylor's Bay, so it seemed reasonable to assume it was Taylor's house.

So who was Robert Taylor? And why was he murdered on this lonely spot?

Local museums are always a good place to find answers to questions, so I called the Great Barrier Museum, and they put me in touch with local amateur historian Bob Harrison, who had once owned the land where Taylor was buried and was moved to give Robert Taylor, whose grave had been unmarked for some time, a proper head-stone.

"The word murdered is quite deliberate," said Bob, "because he was a murder victim." Bob felt it unjust that although many people had heard of the killers, Caffrey and Penn, few remembered their victim, Robert Taylor. Apparently, Taylor had been a popular local landowner. He had around 170 acres of bush and farmland, and also ran a woodcutting operation in partnership with his son-in-law, Fred Seymour (married to Taylor's daughter Elizabeth), who lived about 16 miles away. He was known to most people as "Tusky" because his four top front teeth were missing, making his incisors look like tusks.

*T*he base of the chimney — all that
is left of the Taylor house

Taylor's killers were ship's captain John Caffrey and his mate Henry Penn, who sailed a cutter called the *Sovereign of the Seas* around the islands of the Hauraki Gulf. They often sailed to Great Barrier with supplies for the islanders and returned to Auckland laden with firewood. Caffrey had been in love with Taylor's daughter Elizabeth, and they were engaged for some time before she broke it off. The story goes that Caffrey blamed Taylor for influencing her, and brooded for a couple of years before he and Penn shot Taylor in his home in a bungled attempt to kidnap Elizabeth and her younger sister.

Back in Auckland, I checked out the Central Library for any information on the murder. The library has indexed most New Zealand murders and was able to supply a list of references for this one. These related to several newspaper articles written in the 1950s and 60s, and a couple of books on well-known New Zealand murders. These versions of the story differ widely: in some, the shooting was portrayed as an accident; in another, Taylor lay on the floor while the murderous pair coldly pumped bullets into him. Some say that Caffrey raised the skull and crossbones on his ship; although other accounts just mention a black flag. Several versions said that the killers were hanged in public on the corner of Queen and Wellesley Streets, although the more reliable accounts confirmed that they were hanged in Mt Eden Prison.

In a recent, more lurid rendition (in a book called *Lust to Kill: Notorious New Zealand Murders*, by Fred McLean), Caffrey and Penn were portrayed as bisexual.

The Auckland waterfront as John Caffrey would have known it. AUCKLAND CITY LIBRARIES A11666

Caffrey was said to be prone to obsessive attractions towards both men and women, and, in this story, he and Penn were former lovers. The book provides a soft-porn scene where Caffrey sleeps with the cabin boy, Bill. McLean claimed that the papers of the day made much of Caffrey and Penn's association, referring to the pair as "bosom pals", apparently 1880s slang for being lovers. According to McLean, Elizabeth turned Caffrey down because of all the rumours of his taking sailors back to the boat, and Caffrey was enraged because Elizabeth represented his last chance at respectability and a family. McLean also claimed that, on the scaffold, the two killers parted with a lovers' kiss.

Missing from all of the accounts was any accurate description of Elizabeth Taylor herself, or any discussion of what charms so bewitched her former fiancé. There were no photos of the face that launched a pirate ship and turned its captain mad enough to murder. However, there was a hint of her attractiveness in a book about the Barrier called *Islands on the Skyline*, written by journalist Molly Elliot in the 1960s. She says that Elizabeth had a fine singing voice and was known as the "Songbird of the Barrier".

With so many differing versions, I began to search for descriptions from last century to compare the facts to the myths. Unfortunately, no court records from this period now survive, so the most accurate accounts of the trials are the newspapers — the *Auckland Evening Star*, the *New Zealand Herald*, the *Auckland Weekly News*, and the *Northern Luminary*.

Taylor's death and the fugitives' dramatic escape made a splash on what was already a very big news day. On Monday 21 June 1886, the *Herald* was full of dramatic tales of the Tarawera eruption a week earlier, and also reported on an attempted double murder on the North Shore; the trial of a woman accused of stabbing a man in the city; and a murder hearing at Russell against officers of an American whaleship. "SETTLER SHOT THROUGH THE HEAD" was the headline.

There was no mystery about who the killers were. They were named straight away as John Caffrey and Henry Albert Penn, both well known on the Auckland waterfront. The mystery which captured the public's imagination (and mine over 100 years later) was, why had they done it? Why had they burst in and shot a man in front of his family?

The daily and weekly papers revealed a tale of unrequited love that had all the elements of a classic Victorian melodrama: murder, jealousy, scandal, virtuous women, fallen women, piracy. The papers followed the murder, chase, capture, trial and execution in fine detail over a period of seven months; there were even detailed diagrams of Taylor's house, indicating where all the shots were

MURDER AT THE GREAT BARRIER.

A SETTLER SHOT THROUGH THE HEAD.

THE REPORTED MURDERERS AT SEA IN A CUTTER.

INFORMATION was received in town yesterday afternoon from Coromandel that a dreadful murder had been committed at Tryphena harbour, Great Barrier Island, on Saturday morning last, by which a settler named Robert Taylor had been shot dead by John Caffrey, the master, and Henry Penn, the mate, of the cutter Sovereign of the Seas. The following telegrams were received relating to the frightful news. The first one to reach town was the following

NZ HERALD, 21 JUNE 1886, COURTESY *NZ HERALD*

fired, as well as drawings of all the major participants. As a result, I was able to piece together a highly detailed account of what happened, and with some clues as to why.

It seems that John Caffrey and Elizabeth Taylor had known each other for around three and a half years. Caffrey was a burly, bearded seaman with a glass eye and gold earring, considered handsome by many. Their relationship lasted 18 months before she broke it off. Some reports saying she was influenced by her father, who wanted her to marry his business partner Fred Seymour.

There were various reasons given for why Taylor did not approve of the match with Caffrey. Some say that it was because Caffrey was a Roman Catholic. However, one witness reported Taylor as saying that although Caffrey seemed a nice enough fellow, there was something not quite right about him that he couldn't put his finger on. And indeed there was another side to Caffrey, a violent, wild streak that came to the fore when Elizabeth broke off the engagement. When she finally turned Caffrey down at her father's home, he said angrily that the next time he went to town he would "return with either a ring or a revolver", and that if she did not marry him, she would marry no one else. He also told the Taylors' neighbours that he "was going to finish them all off", and several times over the next two years he threatened both Robert and Elizabeth directly with a pair of pistols.

Elizabeth was quoted in the *Herald* as saying that although Caffrey could be kind "he was always very eccentric and annoying, and he was very jealous. He was in the habit of reading the *New York Police News*, and literature of that sensational description, and he often said that if he ever did anything he would make for New York, and that he would never be taken alive." The *Herald* also reported that a few years earlier in Australia, Caffrey had threatened the captain of the ship he was working on, demanding his wages in advance. Caffrey held a revolver and threatened to blow the man's brains out unless he paid up immediately.

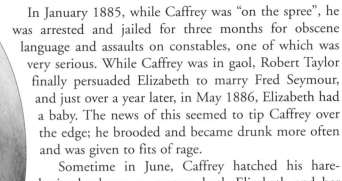

John Caffrey. AUCKLAND WAR MEMORIAL MUSEUM C17391

In January 1885, while Caffrey was "on the spree", he was arrested and jailed for three months for obscene language and assaults on constables, one of which was very serious. While Caffrey was in gaol, Robert Taylor finally persuaded Elizabeth to marry Fred Seymour, and just over a year later, in May 1886, Elizabeth had a baby. The news of this seemed to tip Caffrey over the edge; he brooded and became drunk more often and was given to fits of rage.

Sometime in June, Caffrey hatched his harebrained scheme to capture both Elizabeth and her younger sister, Sarah Jane. It was later claimed in court that he had planned to keep Elizabeth as a slave and sleep with Sarah Jane, and had said that, if they gave him too much trouble, he would shoot and throw them overboard. He bought a chart of the South American coast, despite the fact that he was almost entirely ignorant of navigation. In the days before the murder, Caffrey took on board a large quantity of food and supplies for Walker Gum Company, supposedly to be delivered to the company's store at Blind Bay, but there was enough food to sustain a group of people on a journey to America. Interestingly, Caffrey owed his employer, Adam Henderson, money — two months' takings from his firewood runs (was he stashing away funds for his exploits?). Henderson had told Caffrey not to leave that morning on account of the debt.

Entering the story at this stage was Penn's paramour, Grace Graham, otherwise known as Grace Cleary and Lizzie Read. A 16-year-old prostitute, just 4 foot 10 inches tall, she had been living on board the cutter with Penn for several weeks, but they had known each other for 10 months and seemed genuinely fond of each other.

The night before they left for Great Barrier, Caffrey and Penn held a party on board the ship with three other men. According to Grace's testimony in court, they spoke freely that night of the planned murder. She said one of the men, Lowndes, held a grudge against Elizabeth and asked Caffrey to put her away. Grace said (naturally) that Penn took no part in this talk, that he had just sat in the corner, playing his accordion. The *Auckland Weekly News* reported Grace as saying, "They were looking at a black satin flag. I asked Caffrey what the black flag was for, and he said it was the death of Old Tusky." Grace claimed that Caffrey said he would go ashore to try and get the girls, and if he did not get them, there would be some shooting done. He said he would take some cord with him to tie the father up, and that he would cut out a piece of either his tongue or his ear, so that he could tell no tales. All three men, friends of Caffrey, later denied in court any talk of the murder. However, Caffrey did admit that he might have said the bit about the tongue and ear.

After the party finished, the others helped raise the sails and left, at around 11 pm. Penn, Caffrey and Grace sailed up the Rangitoto Channel in the early hours of Friday morning. This was a perfect time for murder, according to the *Herald*: "The pair knew that there would likely not be any communication with town until next Thursday's steamer, and this would allow them plenty of time to get clear."

Grace and Penn stayed on deck till around 5 am, then went below to sleep. Caffrey came up, but drifted off to sleep, and they woke up with the ship grounded on Rangitoto rocks. They had to wait until the next afternoon to get off, which they did with the help of crew from a passing vessel. Grace said in court that Caffrey thought one approaching boat was a police vessel and took out three revolvers and loaded them, saying, "If they come on board, they'll not get off alive."

However, they eventually arrived at Great Barrier in the early hours of Saturday morning. As they passed Watchman Island, Caffrey tested the revolvers by firing them over the side, six shots out of each. One revolver was misfiring, and would discharge only occasionally.

Once in Tryphena Harbour, they hove to and waited till just before sunrise. Grace said that Caffrey had three cups of straight brandy out of an enamelled mug, but that Penn had nothing to drink. It appears that Caffrey then put two revolvers in his pockets and Penn put one in his, although Grace testified that Caffrey had all three guns. They also strapped on sheath knives and took some cord to tie up Taylor and Seymour. Next the pair got into their dinghy and rowed ashore. Grace saw them go up a small hill (behind which was Taylor's house), wait for quarter of an hour, then disappear over the top.

In the house that morning were Robert Taylor, aged 54; his wife; their son, Lincoln, aged 15; their daughter Elizabeth, aged around 24; her baby Stenton; and their other daughter, Sarah Jane, aged 16. Elizabeth slept in her mother's bedroom with her sister and mother, her father slept in an adjoining room, and her brother, Lincoln, was in another.

At around 7.30 am, Robert Taylor was in the kitchen with Sarah Jane cutting up a sheep with a meat axe, while Mrs Taylor was at the kitchen door. Lincoln was outside, and Elizabeth was sitting up in bed in her nightclothes with the baby. Both Lincoln and Mrs Taylor noticed Henry Penn approaching the house with his hands in his pockets. He came to the door and asked Mrs Taylor if he could buy some butter. (This was not unusual as the Taylors often sold butter to local sailors.) Taylor invited Penn in and told him to wait a few minutes while he went into the dairy. Penn sat down to wait in the kitchen, his hands still in his pockets.

Without warning, John Caffrey burst in through the half-open door, carrying two American Bulldog revolvers. Penn also pulled out a revolver from his pocket. Robert Taylor was then in the doorway between the dairy and kitchen. "Put up your hands, Taylor," said Caffrey. Taylor hesitated and Caffrey repeated the command. Taylor said, "Oh, Johnny, don't shoot me," and then rushed at Caffrey. He caught Caffrey by the left wrist, and young Lincoln grabbed the revolver in that hand and tried to prise it from Caffrey's grip. Caffrey hit Taylor several times on the head with the other revolver in his right hand, and Taylor let go. Meanwhile, Penn had been keeping Mrs Taylor and young Sarah Jane away from the struggling trio.

Lincoln got one of Caffrey's guns free (leaving Caffrey with the gun that was misfiring), threw it onto the ground, and ran into his father's room. Caffrey fired off a shot between the Taylors. Two days before his execution, Penn was quoted in the *Herald* as saying, "When Caffrey fired the first shot a sort of frenzy seized me. I never premeditated killing anyone."

Taylor turned and ran into his room, and as he did so both Caffrey and Penn fired at him, but missed. Taylor either slammed the door shut or fell against it. Meanwhile, after the first shot, Sarah Jane had run through her father's room and into Elizabeth's room. Elizabeth had heard the commotion, recognised Caffrey's voice and knew he would be coming for her in a matter of seconds, so she left her baby Stenton wrapped up in blankets under the bed for safety and climbed out the window with her sister. They ran and hid in some nearby toetoe, with their brother Lincoln close behind them.

Eventually, Caffrey and Penn forced Taylor's bedroom door open, and Caffrey rushed in first, intent on finding the women. But Taylor grabbed hold of Caffrey, who, struggling to make the father release his grip, carried him through into the girls' room. Penn later said that Caffrey had been trying to shoot Taylor during this struggle, but his gun was still misfiring.

As Caffrey reached Elizabeth's room, he broke free from the bleeding Taylor. He looked around for the girls, saw they weren't there and heard the baby crying. Turning round, he saw Penn with his left arm around Taylor's neck and the gun to his head. Penn fired and Taylor fell to the floor, dead. Caffrey said, "Here's a fix, see what's done, and she [Elizabeth] has got away after all. Let us hurry as quickly as possible and prevent her getting away altogether."

Mrs Taylor, meanwhile, who was stout and asthmatic, was running away screaming, and Caffrey told Penn to go and stop her. Penn caught her in the stockyards and menaced her with his gun, saying he would blow her brains out unless she told him where the girls were. She said she didn't know and begged Penn to spare her life. Penn carried on circling her, swearing and trying to get her to say where the girls were. He continually said that she was lying, that she had hidden them somewhere, that he would blow her brains out if she didn't tell. Elizabeth and Sarah Jane could see this going on from their hiding place.

Caffrey, who had left the house via the kitchen door, ran up a gully and searched the surrounding area for the girls. He went back inside and looked under the beds for them, noticed the dead Taylor, then stood outside the kitchen door. He said in his confession that he was there for a minute or two and was strongly tempted to shoot himself, "So vexed I was at what had happened." But he noticed Penn and Mrs Taylor. By this time they were on the beach, and Penn was still threatening to shoot her. When Caffrey ran up, Mrs Taylor said, "Oh, Johnny, this man is going to shoot me." Caffrey said to Penn, "Don't meddle with the old woman, she's never done me any harm."

Mrs Taylor later said that she cried, "Oh, Johnny, what have you done?" and Caffrey replied, " I have done it now." Mrs Taylor responded, "Oh, Johnny, you have killed an innocent old man," and Caffrey replied, "No, he was a bad old [expletive]." Caffrey then said he was not finished yet, that he was going to "finish off the lot at Haratonga" (where Seymour lived). Both men then ran over the hill towards Sandy Bay, where they waded out to their dinghy and rowed back to the *Sovereign of the Seas*.

Caffrey next committed the serious crime of barratry, by stealing his employer's ship (he could no longer claim he was transporting goods to the island). He hoisted a black

The Taylor house. GREENSTONE PICTURES

flag and made ready to sail round the island to Haratonga, which meant they had to sail out into a howling gale.

Mrs Taylor had returned to the house and found her husband dead. She laid him out, then, in a state of deep shock, staggered out to find the girls and Lincoln. They all piled into a rowing boat and headed across the harbour towards the local post office. While on the way, they saw the *Sovereign of the Seas* also beating across the harbour, and could see that it was flying a black flag. They were afraid that Caffrey would run them down, so they kept the boat well to windward and made it to the post office. There was no telegraph there in those days, so Lincoln rode 16 miles on horseback to Fred Seymour's place to raise the alarm.

As Lincoln left, the postmaster, Mr Blair, also launched the cutter *Tairua* to go for help, but they were chased by the pirates and driven back to port. (The *Sovereign* was a very fast ship that had won many Auckland regattas.) Seymour, once Lincoln had warned him, had more luck, and reached Coromandel by boat, where he telegraphed Auckland. Back on the Barrier, groups of armed locals patrolled the beaches, as described by the *Herald*:

> The indignation of the settlers is very great, and should the murderers show themselves in any of the bays, they will be shot down like dogs. It is well known that Caffrey will never be taken alive, as he has often said that he would destroy himself rather than be taken. When he is brought to bay there will be a desperate struggle. He was a great admirer of the Kelly gang and their doings.

The *Sovereign* was out in atrocious weather, and was forced to stay close to the island. It sat for a day or two off Haratonga, where Seymour lived, and observed him return in

93

his boat from Coromandel. The *Herald* reported that the *Sovereign* made ready to attack, but, as those on board Seymour's boat were well armed, the pirates thought better of it.

When the weather cleared, the *Sovereign of the Seas* had disappeared. There were many reported sightings, including one supposedly of Caffrey in the Waitakere Ranges. Six days after the murder, the government offered a reward of 200 pounds for the capture of the pair, or 100 pounds for information as to their whereabouts.

It was soon revealed back in Auckland that Caffrey and Penn had been making cryptic comments for weeks about how they were going to be gone for some time, and people would be hearing about their exploits soon. Penn and Grace had had a meal in a local restaurant, and, as they paid, Penn said, "That's the last threepence you'll see from me for a while."

Out there on the water, Caffrey was having trouble holding the *Sovereign* on his quest to reach South America. Despite his lack of navigational knowledge, he had figured that, if he travelled continually east, he was bound to hit the huge continent sooner or later. But a storm had blown up and Caffrey was nearly killed when he was hit by the boom. They were blown further north, then when they met the northwest trades were forced to go west. Caffrey switched destinations for Tasmania, but eventually they were beached in New South Wales. On the way they made some attempt to disguise the ship by painting it black above the water line, and painting out the first four letters of *Sovereign* to leave the name *reign*.

Grace later said that they followed the tracks of birds to reach land, that she had worn men's clothes and had thoroughly enjoyed herself. She also said that Caffrey seemed depressed, every now and then he would loudly lament what had happened, and would say things like, "Old Tusky must be pretty stiff by now." He also said that you couldn't trust a woman, and perhaps it was better for them to shoot Grace. After that, she and Penn slept with a loaded revolver.

After reaching land, the trio quarrelled again, and Caffrey headed off on his own. However, all three were soon captured by the Australian police and jailed in Sydney, where the two men were charged with the murder, and Grace as an accessory. They were brought back to Auckland and put on trial, arousing intense public and media interest. There were 2000 people in and around the courtroom when the defendants first stood trial, and crowds packed the wharves and streets to see them disembark in chains after being brought back from Sydney. What is also evident is that there was some public sympathy for Caffrey as he had long been a popular figure on the Auckland waterfront, and many said that the murder was quite out of character.

All pleaded not guilty, both Caffrey and Penn putting the blame on each other for firing the fatal shot, and both said that they had no worse motive than kidnapping in mind when they went to Taylor's. Grace supported Penn's version of events, and, halfway through the trial, she was released and became a prosecution witness. She still supported Penn, but in the end it was her evidence that helped convict them both. Because of the laws of the time, neither defendant was allowed to give evidence in their own defence.

After one hour and twenty minutes' deliberation, the jury returned a verdict of guilty for both men, although the foreman stunned the court with a recommendation for mercy. The *Herald* reported that one juror had held out against the others, who were all in favour of a guilty verdict. This single juror argued that, as only one shot killed Taylor, only one of the men must be guilty, and as it had not been proven who had fired the fatal shot, it was better to give both the benefit of the doubt. The other jurymen "weary of the case, eager to get to their homes on a Saturday night, frightened that if they did not bring in a verdict they would be locked up again, were weak enough to agree to the compromise that both prisoners should be recommended to mercy".

Disregarding this unusual plea, the judge sentenced the two men to death. He said that he was obliged to pass the recommendation for mercy on to the Governor, but doubted that it would be upheld. This proved to be true, and the sentence was carried out on 21 February 1887. This was despite a last-minute confession by Penn that he had fired the shot that killed Taylor.

> Penn made a statement and so did Caffrey, but these did not harmonise, and the discrepancies were pointed out to the men. Penn thereupon made a fuller and complete statement, admitting his full share in the murder. Caffrey was so pleased with Penn's frankness that he wrung his hand and said, "Now that you have told the truth like a man, I am ready to go to the scaffold with you."

The *Herald* concluded:

> Both men broke down and cried together, becoming from that moment reconciled and fast friends until they ended life together on the gallows. Both men died admitting their guilt, and the justice of their sentence.

They appeared to be in an ecstatic, trance-like state and as they were taken towards the scaffold, they greeted the warders, clergymen and policemen warmly, and before the trapdoor opened both swayed lightly to the sound of a hymn being sung. And it seems the two did indeed kiss on the scaffold. Here's the *Auckland Evening Star*'s version of the event:

> As the two men thus turned and faced each other, their arms already pinioned, the most affecting part of the solemn scene took place, Penn suddenly stepping forward and kissing Caffrey, who bent forward to receive this last salute and token of reconciliation.

This is the only suggestion I could find that Caffrey and Penn might have been gay or bisexual — apart from the supposed mention of them being "bosom pals", which I could not find anywhere, and one line in the *Herald*, where Mr Napier, Penn's defence counsel, addressing the jury, said:

> Penn stated that he was on terms of the most intimate kind with Caffrey, who had employed him, and had a great influence over him. Caffrey was an experienced sailor, and that gave him further influence over Penn.

However, the word "intimate" did not mean the same then as it does today — it was often used to signify a close friendship. So, on the evidence so far, the case for the pair's homosexuality seemed quite flimsy.

I now knew the main details of the story, and had some idea of Caffrey's motives — jealousy and rejection have been the siblings of obsessive, strange behaviour since the dawn of time. But there was something about this case that made me think there was more to it. There were many in Auckland who felt that, in the light of Penn's confession, Caffrey's sentence should have been commuted to life imprisonment; and a petition had been passed around in support of Caffrey and was signed by hundreds of people. Even Mrs Taylor wrote to the pair in prison, saying that she forgave them for the murder. And prayers were being said for their souls in many local churches. Obviously, many people liked Caffrey, and his violence was reported as being out of character with how many people found him. And how could Elizabeth have contemplated marriage in the first place if the violence was normal behaviour? And what drew Penn into this? It didn't quite add up to me, though, again, the newspapers weren't short on both background and speculation.

The *Herald* reported that John Caffrey had a background of family instability. He was born in a township called Caven, in England, and left London as a three-week-old infant with his parents. His father belonged to the 37th Regiment of the New Zealand Fencibles. Caffrey's father served as a master tailor in the regiment for 21 years, and retired with a pension.

> He was a man with a very violent temper, a failing which his son inherited. The family settled in the cottage and acre at Onehunga allotted to them. Some time after, Caffrey's father took to drink, and in a fit of melancholy over domestic troubles, committed suicide.

Other character sketches were given by someone called Eggington, a former mate of the *Sovereign*:

> Caffrey was a man of unbridled passions and stubborn determination . . . he had for some time been very restless and unsettled in his mind, he never seemed to sleep; and the least drop of intoxicating liquor sent him beating his head against walls and otherwise demeaning himself like a madman.

In an article in the *Evening Bell* printed after the hangings, Neville Forder writes:

> William [sic] Caffrey was a fine stamp of a man, typical of a fine class of men of whom Auckland had reason to be proud . . .

Penn, on the contrary, was a very different character:

> . . . flash undersized runt of a fellow of about 24 . . . one of those undersized, ill-used looking individuals who appear to be always snivelling, and after he took up the calling of a seaman he affected the "Jolly Jack", wore a flaming handkerchief instead of a collar and tie, drank rum and courted the company of the very lowest type of larrikinesses.
>
> The day straight-going Bill Caffrey took Harry Penn as a shipmate he signed his own death warrant and threw away the years of character gained by years of honest toil . . . you'd

never dream that the fine, upstanding "Captain" Caffrey should fall under the influence of such an Iago as Penn. That he did, to his utter undoing, was proved in the dreadful tragedy that ensued.

The *Herald* also described how Penn came from a good family from Milford Street, in Ponsonby, and was married with two young children. However, two years before, he had left his wife and family, donned a sailor's scarf, and given way to drink and easy women.

Of Elizabeth's character, little is revealed in the newspapers, and the line drawings of her in court show only a plain, almost frumpy woman. But there's a hint of another side to her personality in the reports of her being cross-examined:

> She had no tattoo mark on her arm. She had once had the initials JC on her arm. She had put them there herself. They signified Caffrey, and he had asked her to do it.

Harry Penn. AUCKLAND WAR MEMORIAL MUSEUM C17390

As well as newspapers as a source for character references, I sought out Rod Seymour, proprietor of the Puhoi Hotel and son of Stenton, Elizabeth's baby. He had a cuttings file on the murder, including a very faded photograph of Elizabeth holding her baby. She was matronly by today's stick-model standards, but finally I could see a warmth and beauty that belied the severe drawings I had seen before. Unfortunately, Rod was unable to find any other photos of his grandmother. He confirmed that she was a singer, and that she used to sing at Fuller's Theatre (what later became His Majesty's in Queen Street). Apparently, the theatres in those days were vaudevillian so, again, maybe Elizabeth was more colourful than generally portrayed.

Rod had little more to add to the story, but had a different version of why Taylor was called "Tusky": 10 years before he was murdered, Taylor had his abdomen ripped open by a bull's horns and his wife sewed the massive wound up with a hair plucked from a horse's tail!

I had one last avenue to check out and with this came the breakthrough I had been looking for. I called an expert on the history of the Fencibles, the retired soldiers offered a pension and land to provide a fighting force to protect the other settlers if it were ever needed. The *Herald* had said that Caffrey's father was a Fencible, so I hoped I might find more on his family background. From this conversation came the missing piece of the jigsaw: John Caffrey had syphilis. He had been in Auckland Hospital with something called syphilitic lepra back in 1873, 13 years before the murder. This explained a lot, probably all his manic episodes, his Jekyll and Hyde nature, his low tolerance for alcohol; perhaps this was also how he lost his eye.

I went to the Auckland branch of the National Archives to check out the Auckland Hospital entry books for the 1870s. Yes, there's a John "Caffery", aged 23, in 1873, admitted for syphilitic lepra. The spelling of the name is different to how it is usually written, although I noticed that it's commonly spelt elsewhere as Caffery, even in the *Herald*. But he's the right age and the patient's occupation is given as "seaman of Whangaparaoa". Caffrey was known to have lived in that area when younger (he worked for a time on Kawau Island).

I was aware that syphilis caused a form of psychosis if left untreated, but I needed expert advice. So I phoned the head of psychiatry at Auckland Medical School, Rob Kydd. He said that tertiary syphilis was one of the most common reasons for admission to asylums in the nineteenth century. The condition was called general paralysis, and also "the Great Mimicker" for its ability to mimic almost every other form of mental disorder. However, back then, the relationship between syphilis and the mental disorder it caused was the subject of controversy, and not clearly understood until the early twentieth century.

Rob said that when Caffrey was in Auckland Hospital, it was probably with a primary chancre — a sore on the genitals, which is often the only outward sign that infection has occurred. Once this heals up, the disease remains dormant for many years until the mental ravages of tertiary syphilis begin.

Of direct relevance to Caffrey are the descriptions in Rob's psychiatry manual of individuals who were previously respectable citizens displaying increasingly anti-social behaviour. They became more coarse, their tact and judgement deteriorated and their moral and ethical control of behaviour was undermined. The manual reports that a cultured and refined individual may be observed to eat his meals in a gluttonous and revolting manner; his personal appearance becomes slovenly; his behaviour rude and obscene at home and in the presence of friends, and brutal to subordinates. It is no wonder that Elizabeth found Caffrey "eccentric", and her father thought there was something not quite right about him.

So, if Caffrey had syphilis, what of the actual killer, Penn? I found something of an answer in the *Herald*, which mentioned the Lock Hospital in conjunction with Grace. I found this to be a city council hospital for VD patients. There's a Grace Graham admitted both before and after the trial with gonorrhoea and syphilis. So Penn may also have had the disease, although at his age, 24, he had probably not progressed to the tertiary stage. Rob Kydd said, however, that there may be some personality changes such as depression and anxiety in the earlier stages. Perhaps, too, in this state he was more susceptible to being influenced by Caffrey's behaviour.

Today Caffrey would have had a strong likelihood of succeeding with a defence of insanity; however, this was some years before the first test case provided the legal definition of insanity and, as mentioned before, no one was sure then about the link between syphilis and psychosis.

After the murder, Rod Seymour said that his grandmother Elizabeth moved to Victoria Street in Auckland, then Franklin Road, and continued her singing career. Fred Seymour died some years later and she remarried. She died in 1955, having never spoken publicly about the murders since the trial.

The killers were buried in Waikumete Cemetery under a puriri tree. It has been said that, as convicted murderers, they were buried standing up so their souls would not be at rest. Although their graves are unmarked, I was able to find the location using the cemetery records. I discovered that, also in accordance with a common superstition about murderers, no grass grows on their graves.

*T*rue to the old folklore, no grass will grow over the graves of Caffrey and Penn.
PHOTO: SIMON YOUNG

"Let them shoot me"

HAWKE'S BAY HERALD-TRIBUNE

ON THE THIRD DAY, Lance-Corporal Russell was shot. A German warrant officer who witnessed the execution says: "The prisoner died very bravely."

There can be no doubt whatsoever that Lance-Corporal Russell, in the midst of his enemies and in the face of death, bore himself with courage and dignity of a very high order.

These are the last lines of a long dedication etched into a brass plaque on a wall of the David Russell Ward in Napier Hospital. A photo of this forgotten hero hangs above the plaque. Sadly, very few people see it any more: just as the memory of David Russell has faded, so too has the ward named after the hospital's former orderly become rundown and disused.

The plaque reveals that Russell was posthumously awarded the George Cross after he was killed by a German firing squad in northern Italy in 1945. The story the plaque tells is one of remarkable courage. Russell was an escaped prisoner of war, who had obtained civilian clothes and was living with an Italian peasant, Giuseppe Vettorello. He was well liked by the local people, and maintained contact with other escaped POWs in the district, whom he often visited on his bicycle. In February 1945, he was captured by an Italian fascist patrol, who also arrested Giuseppe Vettorello on suspicion of harbouring Russell. They were taken to the company headquarters of the local German commander, Oberleutnant Haupt, at a village called Ponte di Piave. Haupt tried to force Russell into betraying Giuseppe, but he refused to do so, denying that he had ever seen him before. According to an Italian soldier who was present, Lance-Corporal Russell was beaten up by Haupt, but maintained his silence. Thanks to Russell's loyalty, Giuseppe was released.

But the Germans were convinced that Russell had been in contact with partisans and other escaped POWs. He was chained to a stable wall and told that, if he did not disclose their whereabouts, he would be shot in three days. He was beaten up again, but steadfastly refused to talk, and when a civilian who brought him food tried to persuade him to save himself, he replied, "Let them shoot me."

And so they did, on 28 February 1945 — and Russell died "very bravely" according to the German warrant officer witness. According to an Italian interpreter present at the execution, Russell even won the admiration of his interrogator, Haupt.

The words, "He was beaten . . . but remained silent" kept echoing through my mind. What secret was he really hiding?

Searching through a number of books, I was able to add to my sparse knowledge of Russell's story. The George Cross was not awarded until 1948, after the facts of Russell's death had come to light during the war crimes trial of a German officer (presumably Lieutenant Haupt). The medal, created by King George in 1941, recognises exceptional acts of bravery, and ranks just below the Victoria Cross. Russell was originally from Scotland, and had lived in Napier for just over a year before enlisting in the New Zealand Army at the outbreak of World War II. One book, by Geoff Conly, said that Russell, after escaping from prison camp in Italy, had used his time on the run to organise the return of escaped Kiwi prisoners to Allied lines by submarine. Was this what Russell was refusing to talk about to the Germans?

His army file gave away little, so I figured that there must be people still alive in Napier who remembered Russell and who could give me a clearer picture of the man and what secrets he had to hide. I arranged for the Napier *Daily Telegraph* to print a request for anyone who knew him to contact me, and was soon winging south to sunny Hawkes Bay. I arrived on the day the article was published, and went straight to the hospital. But after a few hours there, I was no closer. No one there remembered him, but some gave me names of retired staff members who might have. One of these — Jack Mansfield — seemed the most promising. I gave Jack a call and a very faint voice said, "Dave? Yes, he was a good mate." Jack couldn't see me that day, but I arranged to meet him at ten o'clock the next day.

While I was wondering what to do next, my cellphone rang. "Are you the bloke looking for people who knew Dave Russell?" said a voice. "Well, I was one of his best mates, I came out from Australia with him in 1938."

At last! I thought. But, frustratingly, the man ("Just call me Ken") didn't want to give his last name or meet me. "I'm just doing this for Dave," he said. But he did fill me in on a lot of gaps. He said that David had come out to Western Australia from Scotland in his late teens to join his brother there, and eventually ended up travelling round Australia for 10 hard years. "On the swag," as Ken put it — doing all sorts of jobs, moving from town to town throughout the Depression years.

Ken and David met at a boarding-house in Port Kembla, south of Sydney, where, like most places then, there wasn't much work. They decided to try their luck in New Zealand after reading in an article that carpenters were wanted here. Fresh off the boat in Wellington, they read another newspaper report about how Napier was now booming after the earthquake, so they jumped on a train to Hawkes Bay. Here they found lodgings with fellow Scot Jim Vannan and his family. Ken found a job with an oil company, and Dave soon began work as a hospital orderly. Ken said that Dave was a very popular bloke and a keen soccer player.

When war was declared, David and Ken both volunteered on day one. Ken was certified A1 by the army doctors and left with the First Echelon, but David was knocked back to A2 grade because of his varicose veins — which made him eligible only for service in the Home Guard.

"Dave was terribly upset he couldn't get away with me," said Ken, "But he got his veins fixed up at the hospital, and headed off overseas with the second lot."

Ken and Dave only saw each other once again, for a few minutes in Crete, during the retreat after the terrible battles there in 1941.

I tried in vain to get Ken to meet me, and to answer some more questions. But he was obviously a very private man, and didn't linger long on the phone. As I moved off again, I got a call to say a letter was waiting for me at the *Daily Telegraph*. The newspaper article was obviously doing its work. I detoured to pick up the letter, which was from a Joy Cowlrick, who had apparently dropped it off that morning. She said that her younger brother Maurie, now deceased, knew Dave Russell very well, and that they had spent a good part of the war together. "Maurie talked a lot about David before he died," she wrote.

This looked very promising and I was soon on my way. Joy lived just up the road from the drill hall where David, and as I was soon to discover Maurie, enlisted. Joy is a sprightly 80-something who still works as a colour therapist, and remembers clearly the one and only time she met David Russell.

"He came back with Maurie from Trentham Training Camp on their last leave before going overseas," she said. "I didn't take to David at first. I thought he was a bit common, a bit of a hard nut." Also, Dave, then aged 30, was 10 years older than Maurie, and Joy thought him a bit too worldly-wise for her young brother.

"Maurie put me straight right away," she said. "'He's gold through and through Joy. You won't find a better mate.'"

It turned out that David actually saved Maurie's life in Crete, during the retreat following the disastrous battle for Maleme Airfield. Thousands of battle-weary men were forced to march through the night over treacherous mountains, many dropping from exhaustion and thirst, and others falling down cliffs in the dark, breaking arms, legs and worse.

Maurie had terrible dysentery and couldn't walk, and begged Dave to leave him behind, but Dave said, "You're not bloody dying here," and half carried, half dragged him over the rugged mountain passes to safety.

Dave and Maurie stuck together until Dave was captured at Ruweisat Ridge near El Alamein and put in Benghazi Camp. This was literally just a huge barbed-wire fence in the desert where thousands of prisoners were kept, sometimes for months at a time, before being shipped off to camps in Italy and Germany. The last time Maurie heard from Dave was when Russell somehow managed to get a message through to Maurie, "For God's sake send us some food."

So, after talking to Ken and Joy, I now had a sense of the man — a hard case, who was physically very strong, someone who made friends easily, and who would never let his mates down. The next day I was in Jack Mansfield's lounge, sipping a cup of tea and hearing his recollections of hospital life in the 1930s. Jack and Dave were both orderlies, before Jack became a hospital telephonist, and was on duty the night before David left Napier to go to Trentham Camp.

"He'd been out till the small hours and had come back to the orderlies' quarters," said Jack. "But he couldn't sleep, he was that excited, so he came up to the telephone room, and we sat up talking all night."

Unfortunately, after so many years, Jack couldn't remember specific details about what they talked about that night, but he recalls that they did reminisce about the many good times they'd had going to local parties. He said that both of them liked a beer or two, and that Dave was a very popular bloke. Money was tight in those days, and orderlies didn't earn much, so on more than one occasion, Dave and Jack actually sold their blood, then bought a couple of flagons of beer with the proceeds!

Jack said that, on that last morning, after the sun came up, they went to breakfast at the hospital cafeteria. "Then Dave said his goodbyes to everyone, got his kitbag and walked down the hill to the station. That was the last we saw of him."

As I was saying goodbye, I asked Jack if he could recall if David had had a girlfriend, but he said that he couldn't remember anyone. Just then my cellphone rang, and an elderly woman's voice asked if I was the person looking for people who knew David Russell. I was!

"I knew David very well," she said. I started to launch into my spiel about what we were doing and she gently cut me off with, "Well, I was his girlfriend."

Ah ha! Her name was Nance Wilson and she had caught the tail end of an item on my search mentioned on the local radio as she was driving in her car. Nance was happy to meet me straight away, and I soon found myself knocking on the door of a neat suburban home. The woman who greeted me was in her eighties, tall, slim, elegant and cheerful. I met her husband Frank, who, she reassured me, "knows all about David and doesn't mind this at all".

Nance Wilson

Nance as the young woman David Russell fell in love with. ABOVE AND OPPOSITE: COURTESY N. WILSON

Over tea, cakes and savouries, Nance told me all she knew of David Russell. They had met in 1938, at a dance at the Forester's Hall. She was immediately taken by his handsome looks, and his Scots accent, "Which became harder to understand as he got worked up or excited about something," she said. David was a fine dancer and literally whisked the young dressmaker off her feet. They soon spent much of their spare time together — at Nance's family home at Meeanee, a few miles out of Napier itself, and on the weekends at dances or the movies at the State Picture Theatre.

On one of these nights out, David asked Nance to marry him, and Nance said yes. But her mother was against the match; "Even though she loved David," said Nance, but he was only an itinerant hospital orderly, with no prospects. But while the engagement was off, the couple still continued to see each other right up until David left for war in January 1940.

I asked her what motivated David to volunteer so quickly for the war, and she said that it was for the cause, he believed in the cause, that Hitler and nazism had to be stopped. She also said that that was what she thought kept him going in those last three days. "He would have thought that, if he had to die, if his death would have advanced the cause, then so be it."

The last time Nance saw David was at Wellington Railway Station, at the end of his last leave, the day before he embarked for Britain and war. "It was all very emotional," she said. "There was a huge crowd, and the army band, and we all sang 'Now is the Hour' as the train pulled out of the station."

By that stage, Nance had moved to Wellington and was working at a dressmakers making army uniforms. She received regular letters from David, full of fun and chat about all the sights, sounds and experiences of new countries. "But he would never talk about the bad things, about the war itself," says Nance. David was persistent in his wish to marry Nance and wrote to her from prison camp, asking her to buy a ring and wear it, "But I put him off," says Nance, "I wanted to wait till after the war, and do it all properly."

Sadly, Nance said that most of David's letters no longer exist. She kept them in a pillow slip for several years after the war, then when she was about to get married to Frank, her mother said that she should get rid of them. "In a moment of weakness I said yes. Now I wish I never had." She did still have a few photos and postcards, all tucked away in a box somewhere, and she offered to dig them out. She had one photo to hand of David and Maurie, taken in Tel Aviv, and it showed a completely different side to his personality than the couple of formal photos I had seen before. Both young men are smiling, relaxed, you can see the extrovert, the joker in David. His face is thin, however, and Nance says that she doesn't like his short military haircut, and that he was more handsome than he looked in that photo.

New Zealand ... tary Forces,
Base Rec...

...30169

O. Box 3644,
WELLINGTON.

Miss. N. Oliver,
C/- Shneideman's,
Cable Street,
WELLINGTON.

18th October, 1945.

Dear Miss. Oliver,

Further information regarding the death of 30169 Lance Corporal David Russell has now been received from the Overseas Authorities.

The Officer Commanding the New Zealand Graves Registration ? which recently visited Ponte di Piave in search of further infromt about the soldier, was given some particulars by a member of the I? Carabineri who was present throughout the circumstances of Lance Corporal Russell's recaptur? This Italian states that, in company several other prisoners of ar, Lance Corporal Russell escaped from ? prison camp near Udine abou? the beginning of February, 1945. The ? were pursued as far as Ponte di Piave and hid with the local Itali? until about the 20th February when, realising the hopelessness of ? p?tion, Lance Corporal ????l decided to try and ???? the ????? from his companions. This he accomplished but, unfortunately, was himself recaptured and interogated. It is reported that he was subjected to a gruelling interrogation to elicit the names and where? of his companions and was l?ft without food and water for some four ? but he refused to speak. The Germans therefore tried him on a char? being a spy on account of ?? being dressed in civilian clothing and carrying a map. They found him guilty and he met his death before ? firing squad on the morning of the 28th February, 1945.

Lance Corporal Russell was buried by the Germans, who erected a wooden cross inscribed with the name David Russell and the date of hi? death. Since then, however, the local Italians, who regard Lance Corporal Russell as a hero, have placed a very expensive and beautf? ???b???? on the ????? ??? ??? ?????? ??? ??? ? place is in the Civil Cemetery at Ponte di Piave, Italy, the locatio? being described by the map reference G8183, Italy 1/200,000, Sheet 6.

May I express my sincere sympathy.

Yours faithfully,

DIRECTOR.

Nance also talked of the day she heard David was dead. "I was at work. I was called to the door, someone handed me a telegram, and that was it." Although devastated, she carried on at work that day. "There were many there who were worse off than me, who'd lost brothers and husbands," she explained.

The telegram was very brief, so she wrote to the Army for more information. "Now look at this," she said, extracting a sheet of old paper from her handbag and unfolding it carefully. It was a typewritten letter from Army Headquarters, which gave details of David's capture and execution, "I've carried this in my handbag every day since then, for 50 years. I used to read it and re-read it again and again."

Nance soon moved back to Napier to live with her family, trying to come to terms with her grief. She became very withdrawn and it wasn't until five years later that she met and married Frank Wilson. At her wedding, Nance wore a string of pearls that David had sent her from Egypt, and still wears them today. I asked what was the hardest part about accepting his death.

"If he had died in battle, I could have coped better I think, but knowing he was held for three whole days and then taken out and shot, it seems such a tragic waste of a life, so unjust."

Nance had tried to find out more about what had happened to David, but without success. "I've always wanted to go to Italy, to find the people who last saw him, but that's never been possible," she says. I assured her that I would do my best to track down anyone who knew David in Italy.

In the meantime, she suggested that I contact an army mate of Dave's called Alf Harbottle, who she thought still lived in Hastings. The phonebook revealed that he did, and on the phone Alf readily agreed to see me. I said goodbye to Nance and Frank, with a promise to contact them again soon, and Nance said that she would search out the photos and letters that she had left.

I was excited about meeting Alf, as now I knew about the romantic side of David Russell, I wanted to know something of him as a soldier. Alf didn't disappoint, with a fund of hard-case anecdotes. Alf and David had enlisted on the same day; David in Napier and Alf in Hastings, but they didn't meet until they'd reached Trentham Training Camp, where Dave, Alf and Maurie soon became good mates, along with another Hastings chap, "Lofty" Hunt. They were all posted to the 5th Anti-Tank Regiment, attached to the 22nd Battalion. Alf confirmed that he was often with David when he went AWOL; on one memorable occasion in Capetown when they were having a good time in the local pubs they almost missed their boat, and both received 28 days CB (confined to barracks).

Alf drew a picture of Dave as an extroverted, devil-may-care personality, someone who would cheerily bowl up to the toughest officers, slap them on the back, ask for a cigarette and get away with it. Someone who, when captured in North Africa, made an impulsive grab for his guard's rifle and tried to wrestle it from him. David ended up with a bayonet wound that bled profusely but wasn't serious. Alf says opinion among the other prisoners there was divided between those who thought he'd done a very brave thing, and others who thought it was "bloody stupid because he might have got us all shot".

Alf and David were separated after both were captured and put in Benghazi Camp, in different compounds, and Alf never saw Dave again. David was soon shipped to Northern Italy and eventually interred in Campo PG57 at Gruppignano, then transferred to Campo PG107 near Udine. Lofty Hunt was with David through this time and the pair stuck together after they escaped in 1943. Lofty later told Alf many stories about their time on the run, but unfortunately he died some time ago.

David and Lofty escaped after Mussolini had surrendered to the Allies in 1943, and Italy was effectively split into two, with the Germans occupying the north and the Allies the south. In the days after the Italian Armistice, before the Germans arrived, many of the Italian prison camp guards had gone home, so thousands of prisoners had simply walked out of the camps and taken to the hills and plains north of Venice. Some made it through to their own lines, but once the Germans arrived, thousands of men became fugitives. They slept in the fields in little huts made of maize stalks, and in stalls or haylofts, moving about while fascist and SS patrols scoured the land for them. At great personal risk, many sympathetic Italian peasant families fed and sheltered the escaped POWs.

David Russell. COURTESY BEPPI MARSON

Back in Auckland, I was on the track of someone who could fill in this next part of the story: a man named Arch Scott, who knew David Russell from the time he escaped until his execution. Arch had won a military medal for his work in helping escaped prisoners in Northern Italy, including a scheme in which 46 men were evacuated by British torpedo boat from beaches north of Venice in the dead of night. However, there was nothing I could find to connect Scott to Russell until I came across an article in the June 1948 issue of the *RSA Review*. Written by Roy Johnson, who had been in Italy with Scott and Russell, it revealed that Scott had recruited David into his escape scheme and that they discussed the details of it at some length.

"So that's what was at stake," I thought. At the time Russell was being tortured, he would have had all that knowledge in his head, and therefore the liberty, and probably the lives of Arch and the other escaped prisoners depended on his silence. Because David kept silent, just a week after his execution, the escape scheme came to fruition. Six ex-POWs made it to safety — the first of 47 New Zealanders, Americans, South Africans and Australians who eventually escaped this way, including Arch Scott who went out in the last boat.

I found Arch Scott alive and well and living in Manurewa, retired after a long career as a teacher's college lecturer. He was also an author, who had written of his war-time exploits in a book called *Dark of the Moon*, where he had devoted a whole chapter to Dave Russell.

Scott told me that Dave's first act of bravery was, in fact, coming back down to the plains after he'd almost made it back to Allied lines. In the summer of 1944, Dave had been up into the hills near the Yugoslav border, to a place called Tramonti di Sopra, where a special British mission had come in to organise partisans and conduct sabotage work. Arch said that Russell could have stopped with the mission and been safe, and could have made his way to freedom, but chose to came back down to the plains, to tell others of the escape route.

Arch also said, "The very excitement and uncertainty of life on the plains appealed to him as well. He often used to say, 'These will be great experiences to have had.'"

David managed to get several ex-prisoners out of Italy via the mission, the last group making it through to Yugoslavia in January 1944. By then, however, the escape route was closed down by German and fascist patrols, and David, along with many others, was trapped on the plains north of Venice, in continual danger of being arrested and possibly shot. For several months, David, Lofty Hunt, Arch Scott and others had tried to survey a clear route back up to the mountains, but the risks had become too great, a fact rammed home when some Italians who were caught on a similar reconnaissance mission were hanged on the trees by the roadside (one by a meathook under his chin — a slow and painful death).

Arch Scott figured that if they couldn't make it out by the mountains, they would have to do it by sea, and he soon began work on a scheme to take several small groups of escaped prisoners out by British torpedo boat (not submarine, as Geoff Conly had written) from the beaches near Venice. With help from Italian and British commandos, the operation was set for around 9 March 1945, on a night when the moon was below the horizon, the period called *scuro della luna* — the dark of the moon.

At first, Arch kept the details of the scheme to himself, so that if there was a betrayal, only he would suffer for it. But he soon brought David Russell into his confidence. They spent some time discussing the details of the plan, and both felt that things were progressing very well.

"Too well," said Arch. The last time they met, David was agitated, he had found out that some fascists had been watching him the night before, he felt them closing in. "By hell, Scotty," David said. "These bastards are getting bloody personal." He repeated the phrase several times, as if it were a premonition. The two friends parted with an agreement to meet again soon. David's last words to Scott were, "So long, Scotty, see you Thursday."

But on the Thursday, a young Italian named Beppi came to tell Scott that Russell had been captured near Vettorello's home by the fascists that morning. David knew where most of the escaped POWs in the area were staying, plus all the local Italians who were active in helping the POWs, and the locations of various Partisan groups. But Arch knew this information and the evacuation plans were safe in David's hands. Three days later, Beppi returned to say that David had been shot at nearby Ponte di Piave.

Arch couldn't believe at first that David was dead. He busied himself preparing for the next dark of the moon the following week, when the first lot of escaped prisoners were taken off the beach. Just two months later, on 2 May, the German forces in Italy surrendered, and Arch Scott was able to go to Ponte de Piave himself to find out what happened to his friend. After speaking to locals who were present at the time, he wrote the following notes.

Apparently, Dave had been a very uncommunicative prisoner, so from time to time they turned him over to the Italian interpreter, one Giuseppe Adria, who tried to force him to speak by his own individual methods.

Nothing, however, succeeded in making Dave talk . . . They brought him here in the afternoon of February 28 at about two o'clock — they tried to make him talk but he wouldn't. He replied: "I will not tell you my job here nor where my companions are."

They led him outside into the beautiful grounds and told him to stand against the concrete wall. He asked for a cigarette . . . and smoked it looking around at the world he was so soon to leave. They asked him if he had anything to say — he shook his head, threw away his half-smoked cigarette and stood up rigidly to attention.

I saw the tommy gun marks in the wall.

They left him there where he fell, and about six in the evening a bullock wagon came along — they bundled the body into an Italian ground sheet and took it to the cemetery and buried it without allowing the gravedigger to open the ground sheet and lay the body out decently.

We went to the cemetery to see the grave — the people had had a headstone erected, and, standing between two Italian Patriot Brigade leaders, we saluted the grave of our friend.

So that was how it ended for David Russell. But there were still so many questions. How was he captured, and why? Was he betrayed? Was it bad luck? What were the "special methods" of torture employed by the interpreter? Also, Arch's version of the story did not have any reference to Vettorello being captured — Arch said that now he couldn't remember what happened to Vettorello.

Arch then produced a video, which he had taken on his last trip to Italy in 1995, which had footage of David's two graves — his original one in Ponte di Piave, which is now an elaborate memorial stone, and the plain white marker in the cemetery in Udine, where his body was moved after the war. The video here shows Arch and his Italian friends walking along stooped over, with their umbrellas up in the rain, looking for David's grave among thousands of other identical ones. There is a shout as someone finds it, then a shot of Arch standing shyly behind David's grave.

So, I was tantalisingly closer to David Russell's final hours, but if I wanted anything more, it looked like Beppi Marson and Giuseppe Vettorello, if they were still alive, might hold the keys. Arch said that he himself had seen Beppi just a few years ago on one of his trips back to Italy, so it was likely he was still around. But he said he had never personally met Giuseppe Vettorello. As it turned out, we were many years too late to talk to him; I discovered he was born in 1881, so he would be long dead now.

Arch put me in touch with an Italian friend who, he said, would be sure to help us — Lucia Antonel, who was the granddaughter of a family who had sheltered Arch during the war, and who had recently done a PhD thesis on the escaped Kiwi POWs. Lucia proved to be a real boon; she spoke good English, already knew David's story as it had been part of her research, and was keen to find out more. She confirmed that Beppi was still alive, and soon found out that he was happy to be interviewed.

While I waited for the results of Lucia's research, other pieces of David's life started arriving from around the world. Nance sent me a small pile of photos, which showed

David and his army buddies in many moods and places — in some of them looking battle-weary but with cheerful faces. Poignantly, there was one postcard of St Paul's Cathedral, with Dave's message on the back describing its beauty, and saying, "I hope I can show it to you one day, Nance." There was also a pile of postcards from Syria and Egypt, which showed some of the exciting, exotic, medieval-looking world that the young soldiers were travelling and fighting through.

Then I received a call from David's nephew in Scotland, who had been sent the *Telegraph* newspaper article by someone he knew in Napier. He had met David as a small boy, when he was training in England and had gone to Scotland on leave. Dave used to walk Andrew to school and seemed "exciting and foreign" to the young lad. Andrew said that Dave's mother had died when he was young, and he had been brought up mainly by his older sister Jessie, Andrew's mother.

Another nephew in Australia sent me a cartoon of Russell's story, from the 1960s boys' magazine, *The Hornet*. The comic-strip sticks closely to the official story, with such embellishments as David saying as he's about to be tortured with a branding iron, "Go away, Fritz, I don't like your face."

I also received a letter from Martha James, whose parents David had boarded with when he first arrived in Napier. Martha wrote: "I have some very happy memories of Dave as he was a real character. He came to be like a brother to me."

Then the package I had been waiting for arrived from Italy — containing some of the last pieces of the puzzle. Not only was there a tape of an interview with Beppi along with Lucia's translation into English, but a video of a memorial service that had been held in Ponte di Piave in 1995, 50 years after David's death. Although all in Italian, the

The memorial service held in 1995. COURTESY LUCIA ANTONEL

video gave a sense of what David still meant to the local people. And it seemed that David had not been totally forgotten by New Zealand. Our ambassador to Italy was at the ceremony; and among the correspondence Lucia also sent letters from a New Zealand soldier named Colonel Vernon Lewis of the Commonwealth War Graves Commission. In 1993, he had arranged for a new memorial stone to be placed on the site of David's original grave in the Ponte di Piave Cemetery.

Lucia had discovered that, until two weeks before David was captured, the German commander in Ponte di Piave was someone called Dieter Buck, whom "the people loved and who never hurt anybody". But then Buck was replaced by the "terrible Lieutenant Haupt. If Dieter Buck hadn't been sent away, Dave would have probably survived," she said.

The interview with Beppi was great. He was about 20 at the time that he knew David, and lived in a small village called Staffolo. David often used to stay with Beppi's family, who treated him like a brother. (This appeared to be a pattern — David had been like an older brother to young Martha James, Maurie Cowlrick and Beppi Marson.) Beppi says that Dave used to help him make the local grappa — sometimes with the help of German soldiers who were friends of Beppi! "I have good memories of Dave," said Beppi. "He was generous and an altruist. He trusted me a lot and told me that I was very strong."

Beppi as David Russell knew him. COURTESY BEPPI MARSON

Beppi had to be strong the night he rescued David from a wine shop several days before he was captured. "That night still gives me the shudders," he says. Beppi heard from friends that Dave was in trouble. He had been drinking with two Germans, including one SS soldier; they had all been singing Lili Marlene when "for some reason they started to quarrel, and what is worse Dave began to speak in English".

Beppi said that he turned up at the bar and tried to talk to Dave, who wouldn't listen, so Beppi punched David on the jaw, put him on his bike and took him away, while his friends held the drunken Germans back, who by this time had begun to shout and shoot. With some difficulty, Beppi managed to get David to an underground shelter in the fields near his house, made him a cup of tea, and told him not to leave the shelter until Beppi or a member of his family told him it was safe.

"But, as usual, he never did what he was told," said Beppi. The next day, when Beppi's nephew went to the shelter, Dave was gone.

"Dave had become very restless and wanted to stay with Vettorello, whom he knew very well. I didn't want Dave to stay with him because Vettorello had been a fascist who later on had changed his mind . . . He went to stay with Vettorello because he wanted to get closer to something, I never understood what . . ."

Interestingly, Beppi said that Vettorello was never taken to Ponte di Piave or interrogated, which directly contradicts the official George Cross citation. I reasoned, however, that it's possible that Vettorello was interrogated in his home after David was arrested in the fields nearby — something Beppi would not have known.

At first, Beppi thought Vettorello was somehow responsible for David's capture, and went to his house and threatened him, but Vettorello convinced Beppi that he had nothing to do with the arrest. Beppi still feels that someone probably betrayed David, although he was never able to discover who.

After questioning Vettorello, Beppi went to Ponte di Piave, 30 km away, to try and find out any news of David. Apparently, Lieutenant Haupt considered David a spy because he had been caught with a map and was in civilian clothes. Beppi found out from friends that David was being held in a villa where he was being tortured, and that the Germans were planning to shoot him.

"Of course, I started to worry both for him and us. If he had spoken, all the people involved with helping allied POWs would have been arrested and our villages would have been burnt down; a lot of families and people were involved. Had Dave mentioned their names, only God knows what would have happened. So it was extremely important that Dave kept quiet, and knowing Dave I had no doubts about this."

I already knew that David was beaten and deprived of food and water, but Beppi says that no one really knows how badly David was tortured or what special methods were used by the Italian interrogator, Giuseppe Adria. He says that Dave was chained up for the three days in a room in the villa (not in a stable, as the "official" version says), and that Adria and Haupt were the only people present.

He was also unable to find the person to whom David said, "Let them shoot me," — although David had previously said something similar to him.

"More than once he asked me, 'What would you do if the Germans or fascists caught you?'", said Beppi. "I replied that I didn't know . . . When I asked him the same question, he said that he would not speak because even if he did they would shoot him anyway, and he advised his friends to do the same in case they were caught."

On the day David was shot, Beppi managed to find a spot outside the villa, but couldn't see anything except the backs of the firing squad: "I could only hear the shots." It was a brave and courageous death; but it did look as though Dave was in some ways a victim of his own restlessness and feelings of invincibility — and Beppi confirmed this.

"Dave was very courageous, had little fear and never thought they would catch him. He had a great self-confidence, but he took things too easily, and above all he took too many risks just for the sake of them.

"But he was a good man," Beppi continued. "He loved his country very much and he believed in the Allied cause. That's why he decided to die for it. I am sure that had he stayed put he would have saved himself, but he wouldn't listen. He had an iron will. He had to go around, to do something, to work."

This selfless attitude is echoed by Arch Scott when he says: "You know, even if Dave had been around for that first mission, he wouldn't have gone. He would have waited for everyone to get out first, and even then he would probably have gone back and looked for more."

I finally felt I knew David Russell — a man who had seen much of the world in his 33 years, and who always faced it on his own terms. An extroverted, romantic, devil-may-care rolling stone, who found his paradise on earth and the love of his life, briefly, in Napier by the sea. History conspired to turn him into a hero rather than a husband. His impetuous nature helped bring about his own undoing, but when it mattered, and under what duress we can only imagine, he kept silent and saved the lives of his friends.

This headstone is felt by many people to be offensive and deserves an explanation, not least because Harry Winiata (or Wynyard) worshipped in the parish church.

Winiata and Packer worked on the Cleghorn Farm in this community. Packer learned Maori language from Winiata and had been invited to be a guest in Winiata's home in the Waikato.

Packer accused Winiata of taking money from his purse which Harry Winiata denied. He offered to lend Packer a pound. Two days later Edwin Packer was found dead and suspicion turned to Winiata who sought the safety of his home territory in the King Country.

Settlers who resented the fact that fugitives in the King Country could evade justice pressured the Government to post a reward of five hundred pounds for Winiata's capture.

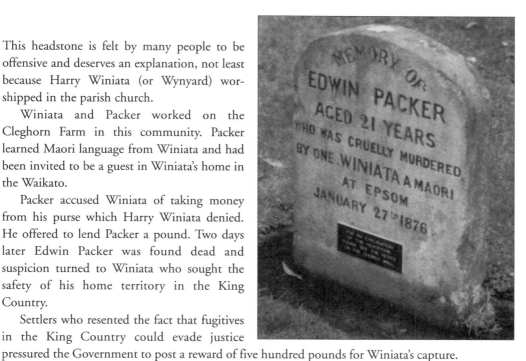

A disaffected prize fighter who had been frustrated in his attempts to buy Maori land seized the chance to gain the reward. With others, he successfully plotted to seize Winiata who was brought to Auckland and tried. He was convicted although the evidence seems to have been circumstantial, and was hanged in Mt. Eden Prison in August 1882. Harry Winiata protested his innocence to the end and was given support at the scaffold by Archdeacon Maunsell and two Methodist clergy.

The careful phrasing of this 'explanation' was in stark contrast to the directness of the headstone and even allowed for the possibility that Winiata may have been innocent. My own journey through the Winiata/Packer story would lead me to believe that at the very least Winiata was a party to the murder even if he didn't actually commit the physical act. I would also end up feeling sympathy for this man, who during his life unsuccessfully tried to straddle the two very different worlds of Maori and Pakeha, ultimately being rejected by both. It's a sympathy I feel uneasy about, though, because there is no doubt that the 21-year-old Packer was cut down in his prime by an incredibly brutal attack with a billhook.

A billhook looks something like a slightly curved meat cleaver, and sometime shortly after 4.30 am on 27 January 1876 at the Cleghorn Farm, Epsom, one of these belonging to the Cleghorns was used with savage ferocity on Edwin Packer. One blow virtually cut his head in two, laying the brain wide open. There was another cut to the cheek and three more cuts to the neck, which almost severed the head.

Not long before this grisly attack took place, Mary Anne Sutton, the Cleghorn servant girl, had looked out her window to see Winiata cross the yard and go into the outhouse where Packer slept. She then heard Packer say, "Hallo Harry, where are you off to?" In another room, Mr Cleghorn's son William was awakened by the barking of the guard dog. He looked out his window, saw nothing, but also heard Packer say the same words the servant girl heard. Within 15 minutes, Mary Sutton was dressed and knocked on Packer's door but received no reply. She returned inside the house and began to light the fire. A little later, William Cleghorn came down ready to go rabbit shooting. He set off with a dog that pointed at something near a stack of posts in the shade of a large hydrangea bush. Instead of finding a rabbit, he found the mutilated body of Edwin Packer. Suspicion immediately fell on Winiata, and the police, aided by local settlers, began a desperate search that would last for the next month until it became clear that Winiata had made it across the Aukati line and into the safety of the King Country. In 1876 this was the domain of the Maori King Tawhiao and beyond European law. Winiata would remain there under Tawhiao's protection for the next six years.

Winiata was described as a handsome man with an athletic, well-proportioned figure, and at the time of Packer's death was 30 years old. He had resided for a long time

The bells at St Andrew's that Winiata rang.
PHOTO: SIMON YOUNG

among Europeans, could speak English fluently and was known to other Maori as Pakeha Harry. He had fought for the government against the Hauhau at Napier. He had embraced Christianity and could quote at length from the Bible. At Epsom he attended St Andrew's regularly, gave money when the plate was passed around and enjoyed ringing the bell for church service. He had also travelled extensively. As a seaman on board the Luna, he had visited all the ports of New Zealand and had travelled to Melbourne and other parts of Australia. Along the way, he seemed to have picked up a string of aliases, being variously known as Winiata Taurangaka, Harry Wynyard, Harry Winiata and Turua. To the settlers of Onehunga, Epsom and the neighbourhood, Winiata was regarded as being always ready to undertake any odd jobs offered him. He had been working on the Cleghorn farm on and off for the past three to four years before Packer arrived.

Edwin Packer was from a small town called Worth, near Barnstaple in Devon, England where his father owned a 1000-acre farm. After leaving England, he had gone to Melbourne, Australia, where two of his brothers were "living in good circumstances". He'd been in New Zealand about six months, having made his way to Auckland by way of the South Island. From a letter found in his pocket it would appear Edwin was feeling a bit down on his luck. "He had only 30 pounds to his credit, felt sick of everything, and being 13,000 miles from his home regarded himself as quite a prodigal son." He was described as having an unassuming manner and a gentlemanly deportment. He was an accomplished musician and spoke three or four languages fluently.

The worldly Winiata and the fresh-faced, homesick, highly educated Packer must have made a strange couple working together on the Cleghorn farm. I traced a Cleghorn descendant, the nephew of William Cleghorn (the man who had discovered Packer's body) and was told a story that has come down through the Cleghorn family that, if true, sheds an interesting light on the Winiata/Packer relationship.

Before Packer's arrival, Winiata was regarded very favourably by the Cleghorn family. He was well liked and trusted, so much so that as well as the work he did around the farm he was given the job of ferrying the three Cleghorn daughters around in the horse and buggy, a job that Winiata highly esteemed. It's interesting to consider the significance of this job considering the Land Wars were still relatively fresh in settlers' memories — a time when settler paranoia about Maori had been at an all-time high. Anyhow into this cosy arrangement walked Edwin Packer with a letter of introduction.

The Cleghorns would naturally feel some responsibility to help out this well-connected, cultured young man. Until he could secure himself a suitable position, he was given the outhouse to live in and Winiata's prized job of transporting the Cleghorn daughters around in the buggy. Winiata was pushed aside. This account included a description of Winiata looking in the farmhouse window one night to see Packer, who had been invited to dinner, entertaining the family with his piano playing. The interloper was now the centre of attention and in the eyes of his peers Winiata had been demoted. Six years later, when Winiata was captured and brought to Auckland, he was met at the train station by William Cleghorn's father, Thomas, who was allowed time to stand aside and talk to Winiata. Apparently, they had a lengthy conversation at the end of which they shook hands. The suggestion was that Thomas felt some degree of guilt at how Winiata had been displaced by Packer.

The other incident that fuelled the tension between Winiata and Packer was Packer's accusation that Winiata had stolen money from him. At Winiata's trial, John Smith, landlord of the Royal Oak Hotel, Onehunga, testified that during the Christmas of 1875 Winiata had purchased several bottles of liquor from him on credit. Smith asked several times for Winiata to pay the bill, the last being about 11 am the day before Packer was killed. At about 1 pm that day, Winiata came to the hotel and paid 1 pound off his account. Later that afternoon, Packer came to the

Edwin Packer

Harry Winiata.
TOP & BOTTOM:
AUCKLAND CITY
LIBRARIES A11864

117

hotel and discovered Winiata had been in and paid off his debt. He went away then returned to the hotel a while later with Winiata in tow, accusing him of stealing 2 pounds 10 shillings and using 1 pound of it to pay his debt. Winiata hotly denied stealing the money, calling Packer a bastard Pakeha. Packer then reported the incident to the police, who went to Winiata's home later that evening when Winiata was just about to leave for a ventriloquist show. He again hotly denied taking the money. While Winiata was at the Variety entertainment, Packer was in the Cleghorns' parlour playing the piano and concertina for the family. It was a hot midsummer night. Packer stayed late before returning to his room. Still dressed in his Crimean shirt and trousers, he lay on his bed in his stocking feet and fell asleep.

There is no doubt Winiata went to the farm early the next morning. He was seen by the maid and William Cleghorn heard Packer address Winiata, and by his own admission he was there. Winiata claimed, however, it wasn't him that struck the blows but a half-caste Ngapuhi whose name was also Harry. It's interesting to note that, although a full Maori, Winiata was quite light-coloured, which adds weight to the idea that the half-caste called Harry was just a cover Winiata came up with when he later found out what the servant girl had seen and heard.

On the other hand, a lad called Vercoe reported a half-caste Maori galloping full speed past Henderson's Mill at about 6:30 am on the morning of the murder. The next day a clergyman and his friend riding along Omaha Beach encountered a half-caste on horseback heading towards Whangarei. He aroused their suspicion by going to great lengths to avoid them. Whether the half-caste Harry existed or not, we will never know, but in the meantime Winiata, guilty or not, decided to make for the sanctuary of the King Country. The fact that he made it is a tribute to his resourcefulness.

After running from the farm, he made his way down the Remuera Road where he met a farmer tending cows. Winiata asked him the way to Orakei. The farmer noted Winiata's light trousers that had a large patch of what appeared to be fresh blood on the thigh. In Orakei Bay he was seen by another man who noted Winiata was wet to the waist. Presumably, Winiata had stepped into the sea to wash the blood from his trousers. Somewhere around Orakei he lay in a gravel pit for five days, only venturing forth at night to steal potatoes from the nearby Maori settlement. He then began his trek south, resting by day and travelling by night. He encountered many people along the way often drawing suspicion but always talking his way out of it. South of Auckland at Papatoetoe he procured food from some men. From there he made it to Mercer, where he stopped to buy food, trousers, vest, hat and shirt. At Mercer he met a small boy and a policeman. The boy said, "That's Winiata," but the policeman wouldn't believe the boy and instead asked our escaper if he'd seen Winiata! From Mercer he pressed on to Rangiriri, where he called in at Shirley's Hotel for a drink and something to eat. The bar was full of Europeans who were suspicious and quizzed him as to where he was going. He said he was heading for the coalmines at Huntly for work. Ngaruawahia was his next stop, crossing the Waikato River by the bridge and keeping up the east bank of the Waipa, then stopping opposite Karakariki and Kanawhanawha settlements before reaching Te Rore. Here he swam the river to the west side and thence made his way comfortably into the King Country.

First reports of Winiata being in the King Country started to appear a month after

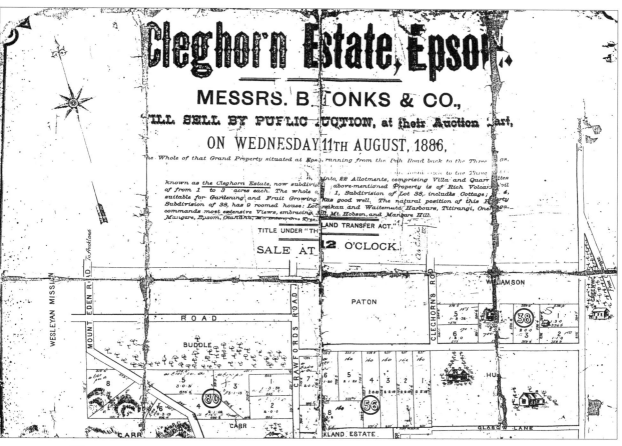

*T*he Cleghorn farm when it was auctioned off, after Packer's murder, 1886. COURTESY P. OLDHAM

Packer's murder, so allowing for a little delay in communications, it means Winiata probably took about two and a half weeks to get there. With 100 pounds reward for his capture on his head, Winiata somehow managed to elude his captors despite the massive manhunt that was mounted to catch him. Keeping still for five days in the gravel pit is probably what saved him. During that time the native settlements in Auckland were constantly policed. The areas of bush around Orakei were systematically searched by a dozen armed policemen 80 metres apart, but to no avail. The Maori at Orakei were fed up with having their whares searched every night and would have been happy for Winiata to be caught.

In the King Country, Winiata made his way to King Tawhiao who asked Winiata several times if he committed the murder. "Are you telling me the truth?" "Are you sure you are telling me the truth?" "Can I believe you that you are telling the truth?" To these questions Winiata replied "Yes, it was a half-caste that done it." "It was a half-caste that killed Edwin." Tawhiao chose not to give Winiata up to the authorities despite repeated pleas for him to do so. Winiata was not the only fugitive from Pakeha justice that the government would have liked to get their hands on. Te Kooti was another, along with Epiha, Hiroki and Pakara. For six years, Winiata stayed at large, living near Te Kuiti where he farmed, raised pigs and grew wheat for the Auckland market. He never let

King Tawhiao who protected Winiata in the King Country.
AUCKLAND CITY LIBRARIES (NZ) A1743

down his guard: he always carried a revolver and was often attended by bodyguards.

During this time, Winiata witnessed the momentous negotiations between King Tawhiao and government officials intent on opening up the King Country to Pakeha settlement and a planned railway line connecting Auckland to Wellington. Tawhiao's insistence on giving shelter to Maori lawbreakers was a barrier to these negotiations. Under Whittaker, the Minister for Native Affairs, there was a "softly softly" approach to Tawhiao. Pursuing criminals into his territory meant the risk of more war, something the government could ill afford during a period of economic difficulty. All this gave Tawhiao considerable mana. But things were to change when John Bryce took over as minister.

Bryce took a much harder line and was prepared to use force if necessary. Winiata had become a focus of settler discontent, for here was yet another murderer escaping to the safety of Tawhiao's stronghold. He had shown the police in a poor light by eluding them in a massive, intense manhunt. Settlers feared for their safety. In 1879 Chief Justice Gillies gave an impassioned address to the Grand Jury about "crimes unpunished" and the "insecurity of settlers' lives and property". Ironically, Justice Gillies would later preside over Winiata's trial. What hope did he have? Winiata had become a political pawn. There were bigger issues than mere justice. Other killers seeking sanctuary could claim political justification, for example the shooting of surveyors trespassing on Maori land. Winiata could claim no such justification. In fact, his act of murder took place right in the middle of an established European settlement. Tawhiao's intransigence over Winiata was a continual embarrassment to the government, so a covert plan was hatched.

Winiata's capture was masterminded by two policemen: Senior Sergeant McGovern of Hamilton, who three years earlier had been involved in the successful capture of Epiha and Pakara wanted for firing on a survey party; and Constable Gillies of Te Awamutu, who, interestingly, was one of the constables who attended the Cleghorn farm on the day of the murder. I strongly suspect the idea was put to these two men by some higher authority whether it would be possible to steal Winiata from under Tawhiao's nose. It's significant that it was at one of the many meetings between government representatives and the Kingites, where Tawhiao once again refused to open the King Country for sale and would not give up Winiata, that McGovern and Gillies approached a half-caste Maori called Robert Barlow.

Barlow was a giant of a man. Over 6 feet tall, 18 stone and athletic with it, he had at various times been a bullock driver, a horse breaker, a bushman and wrestler. He was also annoyed that the King Country was not opening up. He wanted land. The bounty on Winiata's head had now risen to 500 pounds. The plan was put to him and he agreed to undertake the dangerous mission. Barlow was established in the area as a trader in cattle, horses and native products. He also bought pigs from the Maori and sold the pork to the Europeans. It was arranged he would buy some pigs from Winiata, then settle the deal with some grog. One batch would be straight whisky, the other would be rum laced with laudanum, which along with a set of handcuffs and other necessaries were all purchased and supplied by the police.

A week later, on 27 June 1882, Barlow and his wife were sitting on the floor of a thatched hut by the Waipa River closing a deal in pork with Winiata the pig breeder. Watching were Winiata's ever-present bodyguards Kingi and Roaparaho. The deal done, Barlow brought out the grog. The bottle of whisky was soon empty and Barlow began doling out the laced rum. It took effect and, before long, Winiata and his companions were in a drunken sleep. Now was his moment.

For Barlow, getting Winiata out alive meant 500 pounds but failure meant his own certain death. Barlow relieved Winiata of his revolver, which he gave to his wife. He then picked Winiata up and carried him away from the whare to where he had three horses saddled and waiting. Winiata was lifted on to one and his ankles were tied together under the horse's belly with his feet in the stirrup irons. His wrists were handcuffed and he was strapped firmly to the saddle. Barlow's wife took the reins and led Winiata's horse while Barlow rode alongside and supported him. It was after midnight. In this fashion they made it to Kihikihi. By this time, daylight was breaking and Winiata was coming to. He broke free from all his ties except the handcuffs, rolled off the horse and attempted to get away. The local constable, Finnerty, came running from the military redoubt and together with Barlow subdued Winiata, who was transported in the constabulary wagon under armed guard to Te Awamutu and delivered to Constable Gillies. From there he was taken by train to Hamilton and eventually to Auckland to stand trial for Packer's murder.

The moment that Winiata's drugged mind began to comprehend that he had been kidnapped and would have to face the Pakeha law he had evaded for so long must have been quite a moment for him. He had attended many meetings between Tawhiao and government representatives. He had seen the frustration and anger in the faces of these representatives as he had walked freely in front of them, unable to be touched. He had listened to the talk of pardons of the criminals in hiding and knew it was just a matter of time before a general pardon became a reality. In fact, such a pardon did become a reality just months after he was hanged. At this precise moment, though, as the horse beneath him, over which he had no control, trotted into Kihikihi he must have known in his heart that all the talk of pardons would mean nothing now. Nevertheless, from Hamilton, Winiata asked to send a telegram to King Tawhiao. He wrote, "I have arrived here: It is for you to speak or act." To his captors Winiata expressed his faith in promises he said were given to Tawhiao by the minister, Mr Whittaker, namely that "all past offences were condoned". However, Winiata would suddenly find that he was all alone. Mr Dufaur, the solicitor acting for Winiata, visited King Tawhiao, who was indifferent to Winiata's fate. He considered Winiata's crime "to be his own and no one else's". Tawhiao said the Kingites were vexed most by the means of Winiata's capture. If Packer's relatives had come and taken him it would have been fair and just, but for Barlow, who pretended to be his friend, who had slept in the same house and eaten from the same dish, to betray him was wrong and treacherous. Tawhiao remarked that both men, Winiata and Barlow, were murderers. Winiata had killed a man over money and Barlow had given up one of his own people to death for money.

Tawhiao denied that any reprisals would take place, but as far as Barlow was concerned he said he should stay away and not come back. It was advice that Barlow took, but he was not to prosper with his 500 pounds blood money. He moved to Auckland and bought a farm, but in fleeing the King Country he was forced to leave behind five horses, 200 pigs, four cows and their calves, along with other stock and the surroundings of a homestead. It was rumoured that a makutu or Maori curse was placed on Barlow. His family would have nothing to do with him, and within a short number of years this powerful and fearless man had wasted away to nothing and died.

Winiata's trial in Auckland was virtually a formality. The judge said that even supposing it was not the hand of Winiata that dealt the fatal blow, the fact that he was present, aiding and abetting was sufficient to establish his guilt. The jury took just three quarters of an hour to find him guilty. When asked if he had anything to say, Winiata stood and spoke most eloquently for an hour and a half. He began,

Then I shall speak as to the goodness of my body. My first word is whether my voice is the voice of a god or an angel. If I have no love there will be no goodness extended to me. I have embraced the gospel of Christianity so that mountains may be moved. If I have no love I am nothing. If I should give up my body to be burnt with fire, and have no love, no mercy will be extended to me. Love is patience, love is good, love is kind; it is not boastful. I have Christianity, I have faith and I have love. I have travelled over all parts of these islands. I have been to Napier and there fought against the Hauhaus. There my hands were full of Maori blood. I returned from there and remained here in Auckland. I met a half-caste in Queen Street. He said he would kill the pakeha who had quarrelled with him. It was he killed the pakeha. I went there in the morning, I looked into Edwin's room, but I saw he had been killed.

Winiata then went on to relate all the events leading up to his arrival in the King Country and finished by telling how, when he was questioned by King Tawhiao, he answered, "It was the half-caste that killed Edwin." None of this, however, impressed the judge, who donned his black cap saying, "it was a foul, deliberate, unprovoked murder. There is but one punishment for a crime like yours and the sentence of the law which awards that punishment it is my duty to pronounce."

In the days leading up to his execution Winiata conducted himself with dignity, praying, reading and writing. He even displayed a sense of humour. When a warder made a remark about the coldness of the weather, Winiata replied lightheartedly, "Yes, it is cold, but it will be warm enough soon." For much of the time Winiata was attended by the Reverend Wallis, who expressed his utter conviction that Winiata, although a party to Packer's murder, did not kill him. On the day of Winiata's execution, it was pouring with rain. Before the noose was placed around his neck he spoke his last words, in a firm voice and without hesitation: "Listen to me you who are here. My hands did not come upon that man." Then he turned his face up to the wet sky, "I am calling you, oh God. I am delivering my soul into thy hands. Oh remember me when I comest into thy kingdom."

After hanging for an hour, Winiata was cut down and buried in the prison courtyard where nine other murderers lay. Over 100 years later, he would be exhumed along with all the other bodies that lay in Mt Eden Prison when the Mokomoko whanau dug up the courtyard to retrieve their ancestor. Just where Winiata's final resting place is I cannot be sure. Although abandoned by his tribe and family, in the days leading up to his death Winiata continued to write to them. His last letter is full of expressions of love to them and finishes with a short poem.

A SONG OF LOVE
O, west winds blow and surround me,
So that I might lament to you.
While in the mist that hangs above,
And floats to you I yet am near;
For I am one deserted by
The returning company of Te Karamu,
Which should have borne me to
The dark current that below does lie.
I stooped down to the Pua
I fell, and I must die.
*   This is all, Winiata.*

Pua is bait to trap birds. What bait was Winiata referring to? Was it Packer's money? Was it the laced rum that proved his undoing? Or was it the whole world of the Pakeha that he so wanted to be a part of?

Although the headstone that began this journey commemorates Edwin Packer, by drawing attention to the man who killed him, Edwin's family have made sure that we will also remember the life of "one Winiata a Maori".

he Last Man Hanged

SIMON YOUNG

IN LOVING MEMORY OF WALTER JAMES BOLTON
HANGED 1957
AN INNOCENT MAN WHO DIED AT THE HANDS OF JUSTICE
MAY THIS ABUSE OF JUSTICE NEVER BE TOLERATED AGAIN
YOUR LOVING SON
ROBERT JAMES BOLTON

EARLY ONE WET WINTER'S morning, the *Epitaph* crew set up beside the crematorium at Waikumete Cemetery in Waitakere City to record my introduction to the Bolton episode. The bronze memorial plaque inscribed with the epitaph above was just a few metres away, but the cemetery management, acting on instructions from the Bolton family, had asked us not to film it. They had nothing to do with the plaque being put

124

there. Instead, I read the epitaph from a sheet of paper as the camera panned round to reveal a man standing behind me with his head bowed — the man who did place the memorial plaque. Officially, his name is Peter Waller, but his mission is to take the name with which he signed the epitaph: Robert James Bolton.

The man I know as "Jim" has claimed since 1987 that he is the youngest son of Walter Bolton. Although he has no official documentation to back him up, his claim has never been challenged. The Bolton family has refused to talk to him and also declined our invitation to take part in our research. Jim believes the secret of his true identity is inexorably linked with the fate of Walter Bolton. As he has dug further into his own background, he has also made a close study of the Bolton case and has become convinced Walter was innocent of the crime for which he died.

Jim has made several appeals to the Governor-General and the Minister of Justice to reopen the Bolton case, but has been rejected. The Justice Department studied his claims but concluded there was insufficient new evidence to warrant a full investigation, let alone a posthumous pardon. Still Jim presses on — eloquently and forcefully stating his case — delving into the darkness of a 40-year-old murder case in an effort to find out who he is. But it's a lonely quest.

"No one wants to tell me nothing, not people in official positions, not family, no one — it's like a block wall, a code of silence. They would say to me things like 'Dig deeper, dig underneath and you'll find what you're looking for,' but they'll never come out and tell me. It's like they're scared."

By his own admission, Jim has had a chequered past. Adopted at barely 18 months old, he spent most of his early life with a foster family in Auckland. He claims he was physically abused, and often taunted about his father. At one stage his foster mother told him his father was "a bad man and he got what he deserved". According to his birth certificate, his birth father is one Ronald MacNeil, a seaman who disappeared after a trip to Panama. His birth mother, Doreen MacNeil, has never been traced, and Jim believes she never existed — a false name was entered in the records to protect the identity of his real mother.

When Jim was nine, his foster parents separated and he started running away from home. By the age of 10, he was placed in a boys' home where he says he was often locked up for 23 hours a day. At 12, he was fostered to a family in the South Hokianga. In his mid teens, he became involved with gangs, and in the early 1980s he was imprisoned for assault. On his release, he determined to clean up his act and put his personal demons to rest.

Shortly afterwards, he had a nightmare that changed his life.

"I'm running through the Auckland Domain in a pair of jail underwear. It was in the 1950s, and I'm going along and everyone's calling me 'Jim'. And I spoke to one person and he said, 'Oh, we thought you were dead,' and I says 'I'm not yet but they're after me and they're going to hang me.'

"Right the way through the dream, I kept trying to wake myself out of it — I didn't want this dream, eh.

"Then they caught me and dragged me back to Mt Eden Prison. I can remember the cold, the loneliness, the helplessness — and I was saying, 'Where's someone to help me 'cause I haven't done anything wrong?'

"Then they gave me this sedation. They virtually carried me up the scaffold. They bound my hands, bound my feet and they went to put the bag over my head. I pulled my head back and looked over at the witnesses and said, 'No! I'm an innocent man and youse know it, so you can watch my face as I die and remember it well.'"

Jim woke up in a cold sweat. Later he discussed his extraordinarily vivid dream with his girlfriend:

"And as I'm telling her, I see her looking at me very strangely, and she said to me, 'Have you heard the news today?' — I said, 'No,' — and she said, 'Well, I have: do you realise it's 30 years ago today that the last man was hanged in Mt Eden Prison?'

"She turned around and said, 'That could have been a previous life,' — and all my childhood memories came flooding back — it was really incredible, all of a sudden this feeling started going through my body that I didn't want; I don't think anybody wants to know their father is a murderer."

That's when Jim began a detailed study of the case of Walter Bolton, executed in February 1957 for the murder of his wife Beatrice. He was greatly disturbed by what he found out, but couldn't get anyone in authority to take his concerns seriously. Eventually, in 1988 in frustration, he poured two cans of red paint over the front steps and doors of Parliament. He then lay down a challenge to several MPs who witnessed his protest.

"I just looked at them and said, 'Clean that up as easily as you clean my parents' blood off your hands — and remember me well because I'm coming back again.'"

Jim was convicted of wilful damage and ordered to pay $10,000 restitution. He countered with an offer of $2000, which was quickly accepted. Jim believes this was proof the government was keen to sweep the matter under the carpet in the hope he would give up his campaign. It was wrong.

In researching this episode of *Epitaph*, I have come to know Jim very well, and I have no doubt he will continue his campaign until he believes it has reached a satisfactory conclusion. Beyond circumstantial evidence, uncanny coincidences and a striking physical similarity to Walter Bolton, he has nothing to prove he is Bolton's son. And yet the strength of his resolve is such that I would like to believe him. Certainly, I hope that the television programme and this book will prompt someone who knows the truth, who knows who Jim really is, to come forward and help a man carrying an immense burden of lost identity.

Although it was beyond the scope of our television programme to prove or disprove Jim's claims, we decided to investigate the Walter Bolton story to see if we could cast any light on a case that continues to provoke strong debate 40 years after the fact. Our first stop was the scene of the crime: Wanganui.

In the early 1950s, the River City was just starting to emerge from the shadow of World War II. There was talk of new industry, new business, new opportunities. Bold plans were afoot for hydroelectric schemes on the Wanganui River. But by the late 1950s, the locals had to face a bitter reality. Instead of expanding, many businesses were relocating and even the town's traditional industries were finding the going tough. The town's young people were leaving in droves, and Wanganui was left with the rather lacklustre reputation of being a good place to retire.

Walter (Jim to his friends) and Beatrice Bolton lived on one of the best farms in the

The Bolton farmhouse. COURTESY CHRISTCHURCH *STAR*

area, Rusthall, just a few kilometres east of Wanganui, on the road to Fordell. It belonged to one of the largest private landowners in New Zealand at the time, Walter Fernie, and Bolton had very successfully managed the farm for over 25 years.

The Boltons married in 1913 and raised six children, all of whom had grown up and left Rusthall by the 1950s. The family was highly respected in the community and Walter and Beatrice appeared devoted to each other. Even though he was in his late 60s, Walter was a strong, virile man who still did his share of the hard work around the farm. By contrast, Beatrice was a tiny, frail woman who seemed obsessed with her health. She consulted many doctors and regularly took medication, sometimes even concocting brews herself. Although the family thought she could be diabetic, her illnesses, both real and possibly imagined, were never serious enough to cause great alarm.

That all changed in March 1955 when Beatrice was rushed to Wanganui Hospital suffering severe vomiting. She recovered in a week but shortly afterwards visited her doctor complaining of numbness; he diagnosed neuritis (inflammation of the nerves) of the extremities but could not find a cause. Beatrice was sick all winter, and although several doctors and specialists were consulted, no one could determine the root of her problem. In September, following another episode of severe vomiting, her gall bladder was removed and her condition improved markedly. Her doctors noted Walter appeared very concerned about his wife's well being — even going so far as to save her vomit for inspection when they made house-calls.

However, in January 1956 Beatrice was admitted to Braemar Private Hospital in Wanganui, exhausted from vomiting and diarrhoea. Her neuritis was so bad she was practically paralysed. A nurse at the hospital said she looked like a concentration camp victim. Her family was informed that she could be near death.

Slowly, though, she recovered, and after five months in hospital, during which time she hadn't vomited once, she was discharged. The same day, she and Walter visited her sister, Florence Doughty, for afternoon tea. Within an hour, she vomited down her dressing gown, and Walter was on the phone to the hospital yelling that they've "sent home a sick woman". It was decided Beatrice would stay at Florence's house in Wanganui while Walter continued to live at Rusthall and manage the farm.

After improving for a month, Beatrice suffered another violent vomiting attack shortly after returning from a visit to the farm. Two days later, 10 July, Walter called her doctor to say she seemed better. Beatrice managed a cup of tea at lunchtime but shortly afterwards started retching and complaining of stomach pains. That night she was readmitted to Wanganui Hospital where she went into a coma and died at one o'clock the next morning.

For Beatrice, a 17-month nightmare was over. For Walter it was just beginning.

A young doctor at the hospital was suspicious and wouldn't sign the death certificate. He knew Beatrice died of severe dehydration but there was no apparent cause. Specialists in Wellington performed an autopsy and found an unnaturally high amount of arsenic in the dead woman's internal organs. Their findings sparked a five-month police investigation, which culminated in the arrest of Walter Bolton on a charge of murder.

In Wanganui, I talked to former Police Constable Roy Knofflock. A tall, distinguished man in his 70s, he welcomed us with a bone-crushing handshake and slight bemusement that anyone was still interested in the 40-year-old case. But when I showed Roy the photo taken of Bolton on his arrest, he started to share his memories.

"Yes I remember this photo, I took it." Roy told me. "Bolton never said a word the whole time, and looking at it today he seems to be saying, 'Who, me?'"

At one stage during the police inquiry, Roy went with Inspector Frank Thompson up the Wanganui River to Ranana to interview one of the Bolton daughters, Grace Cook. Grace had been estranged from her parents for 20 years because of a dispute over her marriage, but had returned to the family home on her mother's 64th birthday and subsequently helped care for her. After Beatrice's death, Grace spent a lot of time at Rusthall with her father. It was in that period that Thompson was particularly interested.

Roy says he was told to make himself scarce during the interview and came back two or three hours later to find Grace obviously upset and Thompson ready to leave.

The photograph taken by Roy Knofflock. NEWS MEDIA COLLECTION

"I didn't say anything on the way back home, you just didn't ask detectives questions, but eventually Inspector Thompson said, 'Well, I think the case against Walter Bolton has just been considerably advanced.'"

Grace Cook would testify in court that she had several long conversations with her father about her mother's death. They discussed the police theory that only two people could have given Beatrice arsenic: Walter or Florence Doughty or both of them. Grace said she couldn't see her father doing it but felt Florence could have because she acted very strangely after the death. Walter would have none of it and suggested Beatrice may have taken arsenic herself.

"I replied, 'No, no,'" Grace testified, "that would be like cutting off your own arm, a piece at a time, no one would do that."

A couple of days later, Grace tackled her father again about her suspicions concerning Florence.

"He was agitated and on the verge of tears and said, 'I suppose your aunt and I did it between us.' I said, 'I don't understand you — done what?' And he replied 'About your mother.'"

Bolton also told Grace he thought he "might have to do a stretch" and later gave her an envelope containing 50 pounds. Grace said she was very angry and felt like she had been "bought".

According to Roy Knofflock, Wanganui was split pretty evenly on whether Walter Bolton was guilty. Although he had never met Bolton before taking his photo, Roy says he was well regarded in town, as a farmer and a gentleman. However, that opinion was sorely tested when a sensational rumour swept the town: Bolton had been having an affair with Florence Doughty.

Even today, Roy remembers how incredulous locals were at this bizarre twist.

"Oh, they wouldn't believe it — he's 68 years of age — c'mon — to go down to your wife's sister? The town wouldn't believe it."

WHEN FLORENCE DOUGHTY APPEARED in court, there was standing room only. An elderly woman, severely dressed in black, her face obscured by large dark glasses, Florence admitted the affair and gave details of her sister's illness, including the circumstances leading up to her death.

Roy Knofflock was in court at the time.

"She would not talk above a whisper. No one could hear her in the court — counsel had to repeat everything she said for the benefit of the judge and the jury. She was a very reluctant witness."

Reluctant she may have been, but her evidence was crucial to the prosecution case. She told the court that on the day before she died, Beatrice complained her cup of tea "tasted queer". Florence reported that Walter said several times the milk was "off" because it had been left out overnight. But Florence swears she put the milk away — in any case her tea tasted fine and she wondered why Walter had made all the fuss?

Prosecuting the case was distinguished barrister Thaddeus McCarthy (later Sir Thaddeus, President of the Court of Appeal). This was his first case as a prosecutor (and, as it turned out, his last) and he knew he had a fight on his hands. Privately, the local police told him they doubted the charge would stick, but he was confident the case would be stronger as the trial continued.

Now aged 89, Sir Thaddeus agreed to an interview and received us in his apartment overlooking Wellington Harbour. Although he protested the case was 40 years old and he couldn't remember many details, it was obvious as the interview progressed that his sharp legal mind was still finely tuned.

"The case for the Crown, in its essence, was that the arsenic could not be self-administered because no sane person could possibly have gone through the agony which she did and continue to dose herself to that degree. On every occasion that there was a violent upsurge in arsenical poisoning, she had been in association with her husband, and if it was deliberate it couldn't have been done by anyone else."

Sir Thaddeus relied heavily on the expert medical opinion of several doctors and the testimony of the country's foremost pathologist at the time, Dr Philip Lynch. Following an exhaustive study of the forensic evidence, Lynch concluded that Beatrice Bolton had received near-fatal doses of arsenic on at least two occasions during her 17-month illness and that the fatal dose had been administered no more than two days before she died.

The Crown sought to prove Bolton had the opportunity to poison his wife and, as a farmer experienced in using arsenic-based sheep dip, he had the raw materials at hand to do the job. And his motive was simple: another woman. With his wife out of the way, the Crown proposed, he would be able to resume his relationship with her sister.

The shed where it was claimed that Bolton refined the arsenic from the sheep dip

The prosecution placed heavy emphasis on the fact that Walter Bolton had been caught out lying during the police investigation. Several times he was asked about his wife's diary but denied she kept one. The police later learnt that, following their inquiries, he rang Florence Doughty and told her Beatrice's diary was in her house. Florence found the diary and burnt it. She said it was a spur-of-the-moment decision and Walter hadn't told her to do it. Bolton consistently told the police he didn't know of any diary until they confronted him with Florence's statement — only then did he admit knowing about the diary and phoning Florence about it.

The police were interested in the diary because one of Bolton's daughters-in-law had told them she had found it and read a passage in which Beatrice wrote, "Now I understand what one means by saying they are broken-hearted." The police speculated this could have meant Beatrice had discovered the affair between her husband and her sister — a situation that could have strengthened Bolton's motive to kill her.

Bolton told police he had spent his life savings of 500 pounds on Beatrice's medical care. However, when police got authority to check his bank account, they found the balance was 2556 pounds. Bolton also claimed more than 1250 pounds found buried in the front garden at Rusthall was money he won at the races; however, other members of the family testified most of the money belonged to Beatrice.

Walter Bolton also lied about his relationship with Florence Doughty. Perhaps understandably, he wanted to protect her integrity; however, the lies were yet another black mark against him. Police gave evidence of a blazing row at Rusthall when Walter arrived to find Florence being interrogated by detectives.

"Don't tell them anything," he said, "not another word until you've seen a solicitor."

Bolton denied he had been more than friendly with Florence and that he had bought furniture for her house. Furious, he demanded to know who had told the police otherwise.

"I did," sobbed Florence

Suddenly, Bolton changed his tune. "Well, what of it? We're only human."

"I only wanted your friendship," Florence cried, "you should not have dragged me down like this."

"Well, I suppose I could have gone up the street and got what I wanted," said Bolton.

He then admitted the affair took place while Beatrice was in hospital during the first five months of 1956, but said it was over by the time she was discharged.

BOLTON'S DEFENCE TEAM WAS led by Brian Haggitt who cautioned the jury that, "We are not here to judge these two elderly people for a breach of the moral code." He said the Crown "was alleging cold-blooded murder over a long period, but common sense said no one would do such actions without a compelling motive".

But Haggitt played what he hoped would be his trump card last. The defence petitioned the judge to allow it to introduce new evidence — evidence it claimed would show Beatrice Bolton died of accidental arsenic poisoning. The prosecution protested the evidence should have been presented earlier, when it would have had the chance to cross-examine the witnesses, but the judge allowed the defence to continue.

"We do not dispute that death was due to arsenical poisoning," Mr Haggitt told the jury, "but we contend that the Crown has not only failed to prove that it was administered with homicidal intent, but has failed to disprove accidental poisoning and has not even investigated that possibility."

The defence called forensic scientist Len Spackman, who testified he had tested a freshwater spring on Rusthall Farm and found it to be contaminated with arsenic. He believed the poison had leached into the spring from the farm's sheep-dip pit, which was located about 50 metres up the hill. The court was told the pit contained about 1000 gallons of toxic dip at dipping time and that it was common practice for the pit to be emptied over the bluff, right above the spring.

The dipping pit is long gone, but the spring is still there, and I inspected it during my visit to Rusthall Farm. There are still rusty old pipes leading from the spring up the slope towards where the old farmhouse was — these are the remnants of a system Walter Bolton built to pump water from the spring to the house to supplement the domestic water supply. Len Spackman testified that water from taps inside the farmhouse tested positive for arsenic. He also tested Walter Bolton for arsenic and found traces in his hair.

The jury inspecting the dipping pit. COURTESY CHRISTCHURCH *STAR*

Prosecutor Sir Thaddeus McCarthy told me he was amazed by the defence claims and immediately went out to Rusthall Farm to see for himself. Later the jury also went out to inspect the spring. Sir Thaddeus said he came to the conclusion that nobody could have drunk water from the spring because it was "so appallingly dirty"; however, the pipes, the pumping system, and Mr Spackman's evidence all point to the fact the contaminated water was used by the Bolton household for drinking, cooking, washing and cleaning.

Len Spackman also gave evidence that he had conducted experiments similar to those carried out by the government analyst, Mr Davis, adding sheep-dip powder to tea, with and without milk. Mr Spackman testified the taste and smell of this tea was "very pronounced". He also repeated Mr Davis's experiment to refine a clear solution from the sheep-dip powder, but it was his opinion that this scientific process would be very difficult for a layman to complete successfully. The defence reiterated that the police search of Rusthall had failed to find any equipment Bolton might have used to refine the sheep-dip powder — and yet the whole Crown case rested "on the claim this old farmer skilfully and diabolically distilled a devil's brew and carried it around with him".

Len Spackman died early in 1997 at the age of 93. His close friend and colleague, forensic scientist Dr Jim Sprott told me Spackman would talk at length about the Bolton case. "He was convinced in his own mind that Bolton was innocent. He felt that he had failed him and he carried that burden for the rest of his life — he never got over it."

Sprott says most people, if exposed to arsenic, excrete it very quickly but he says Spackman believed Beatrice Bolton was one of a small percentage whose body couldn't get rid of the poison and instead stored it in the liver. If something happened — a sudden shock, excitement, change of diet, etc. — then the arsenic could suddenly release causing severe illness and possibly death. This was Spackman's explanation for why Beatrice recovered when she was in hospital but relapsed when she returned home. Spackman believed that, although other members of the Bolton family would have been exposed to the contaminated water at Rusthall, they excreted the arsenic quickly and so didn't get sick. But tiny, frail Beatrice, who led a sedentary lifestyle inside drinking large amounts of tea, steadily added to the arsenic in her system till the toxic shock killed her.

The Crown couldn't prove Walter Bolton poisoned his wife — it could only show he had the opportunity and motive to do so. The case stood or fell on which forensic evidence the jury believed. On this score Jim Sprott is particularly scathing.

"Juries consisting of lay people, with respect, can't be expected to understand the intricacies of forensic evidence that would tax even the expert. So then what does it come down to — how do juries decide who's right? By the colour of my tie, the cut of my suit? Plainly, forensic evidence is not absolute — no matter how convincingly the evidence is presented. And when a person's life depends solely on forensic science — well, Arthur Allan Thomas would be dead and he was innocent; Murray Kessel would be dead and he was innocent; so would Colin Burt and Lindy Chamberlain. And that would all be down to forensic science."

Summing up the case at the end of Bolton's trial, Judge Gresson spent considerable time going over the prosecution and defence cases. Essentially, he reduced the jury's options to two: either it accepted the defence of accidental poisoning; or it found Walter Bolton guilty as charged.

On 7 December, the jury retired to consider more than 600 pages of evidence presented during the nine-day trial. Prosecutor Sir Thaddeus McCarthy remembers the atmosphere on the final day was extremely tense and emotional. But, in the event, no one had to wait long — in just over two hours the jury returned with its verdict: guilty. Judge Gresson asked Bolton if he had anything to say before sentence was passed.

"I plead not guilty, sir," Bolton said in a high-pitched voice.

The death sentence was mandatory for murder and was duly passed on Walter Bolton. The judge then rose and, as tradition dictates, everyone in the court stood as he left. But Sir Thaddeus told me that defence counsel Brian Haggitt was "so spent he couldn't get up — he just sat there slumped at his desk.

"It was one of the most emotional things, I think the most emotional thing in my career, all my years in law, which is most of my life. But I say, and I say again and again, he got a fair trial."

Former Police Constable Roy Knofflock told me of a certain publican in town whose hotel was only a short distance from the Supreme Court. This publican took a strong interest in the case and attended the courtroom sittings as often as he could. He was absolutely convinced Bolton was guilty; in fact, he started to take bets on the verdict, and according to Roy he made a lot of money. When Bolton was convicted and condemned, the publican said, "Don't pay me — I'll bet you double that he hangs."

Walter Bolton lodged an appeal alleging misdirection by the judge. Sir Thaddeus says the appeal was discussed at a high level inside the government, however, it was decided to let justice take its course. The deciding factor was the length of Beatrice Bolton's agonising illness — the result of a calculated and callous campaign by her supposedly attentive and caring husband.

AT SIX O'CLOCK ON THE evening of 18 February 1957, they came for Walter Bolton. He was so heavily sedated, he had to be carried up the steps to the scaffold. He was asked if he had any last words. He didn't — and he swung into eternity.

There is a widely held belief that the execution was botched: the hangman miscalculated and Bolton didn't die instantly but slowly strangled to death. There is also a story he was hanged sitting on a chair. Neither of these stories is substantiated by police eyewitnesses. Bolton's death certificate records clearly that he died of a broken neck caused by hanging.

He was cremated and his ashes returned to his family in Wanganui. He was buried in the picturesque Aramoho Cemetery in the same plot as his infant daughter Lexie and Beatrice Bolton, the wife he was convicted of murdering.

I visited the grave with the man who started the story with his memorial plaque in Waikumete Cemetery in West Auckland, the man who signed the plaque Robert James Bolton. He has no doubt the Wanganui gravestone is a telling reminder that this story is not over.

"It shows that someone else also knew that he hadn't murdered her because if they had then they would never have put them together — that would have been sacrilege to all things.

"I can never bring my father back, I can never go back and replace my life. But I can honour him and that I swear I'll do so they both may rest in peace."

"Jim" at Walter Bolton's grave.

Jim's search for his identity has uncovered many interesting leads, some of which do indeed suggest that Walter was his father, but Jim still has scores of questions to answer. His quest is far from resolved and would make a chapter in its own right. He may even uncover further facts about the poisoning of Beatrice.

It is generally accepted, however, that the outcry that followed Walter Bolton's execution, and the lingering suspicion he may have been innocent, caused the government to lose its stomach for hanging. The noose was never used again, and in 1963 Parliament voted to abolish capital punishment. Too late for Walter Bolton — he will always be remembered as the last man hanged.

B*roken Heart*

WHEN I FIRST HEARD about this grave in Westport, I was told the inscription read "died of a broken heart". After my first phone call I discovered this was not true. However, the woman at the information centre knew which grave I was referring to — that of a man named Anders Andersen — and it seems that although his inscription doesn't say so, locals still know of him as the man who died of a broken heart.

I found the grave in Orowaiti Cemetery in Westport. The actual inscription reads:

ERECTED BY THE CITIZENS OF WESTPORT TO THE MEMORY OF
ANDERS ANDERSEN
A VICTIM OF INJUSTICE
DIED 14TH OCTOBER 1908
BORN AT KOLBJORNSVIG, NORWAY, 28 FEB 1877

Who was this man so far from home, and what injustice had occurred to cause his death and the strong feeling of the people of Westport?

I ordered a copy of Andersen's death certificate from Births, Deaths and Marriages and looked at the cause of death, expecting a murder or perhaps a hanging. Instead I discovered that Anders Andersen had died of epilepsy. Not exactly the dramatic death I had envisaged, a death that had caused a whole town to raise money for his gravestone. If his death was from natural causes, what then was the great injustice?

I checked the local papers for the day of his death, and found what I was after in the *Greymouth Evening Star*. There was a small article referring to Andersen's death, but it was the main headline that pointed to the bigger story hinted at in Andersen's epitaph. It seemed our Norwegian sailor had been involved in a manslaughter case — a case that was, at the time, the longest running trial in New Zealand's history.

Looking through earlier copies of the newspaper, I found many more headlines referring to the 'Westport Murder Case'. It seemed the Westport saga began with another death on a Friday night in May 1908.

Anders was 31, a Norwegian with fine features. He and his mate Olaf Hallinen were seamen off the SS *Canopus*, which was in the busy port of Westport loading coal. On this night they went ashore planning to sell some of their uncustomed tobacco. During

The busy port of Westport as it was in Anders' day. ALEXANDER TURNBULL LIBRARY F15412 1/4

books regarding the Westport murder trial, so took a trip to the library. I found more books than I expected. A chapter about the trial appeared in *New Zealand Sensations* by Rex Monigatti; it also features in *Random Recollections*; there was a short extract in *The Longest Beat* by Kit Carson and Yvonne Davison; and the final chapter of *Hanlon* by Ken Catran was devoted to the case. I found a contact in Westport who also sent me various news articles that have appeared about Andersen and Hallinen over the years. It was with one of these envelopes from Westport that I received my first photo of the two seamen.

*A*nders and Olaf.
COURTESY DAN MALONEY

Olaf Hallinen looked like his name: big and solid, and he had a protective arm behind his mate Anders Andersen. Anders was seated and looked a bit more well-to-do with his bowtie and pinstriped suit.

In the papers, the headlines on the case appeared regularly. It seemed the case continued purely on the testimony of the 18-year-old Connelly; and all along Connelly refused to take the rap for any part of the murder, despite evidence that Bourke's pipe had been found in his possession upon his arrest.

A quick flick through the *Police Gazette* before 1908 soon made things pretty clear to me. At only 18, Connelly's name was already mentioned several times for convictions and terms of imprisonment for drunkenness, fighting, stealing and obscene language. It was plain to me that Connelly's version was just a cover up, his idea to blame the foreigners originating from the night he spent with them in the police cell. But obviously the jury didn't share this opinion. The verdict found both Andersen and Hallinen guilty of manslaughter and sentenced them to seven years' hard labour at Wellington Gaol. It had been Connelly's word against theirs, and the jury had chosen to side against the foreigners.

The seamen were shocked, but most outraged was the pair's defence lawyer, McDonald. He described the proceedings to the papers as a "comic opera", and asked how a man declared likely to be the sole murderer by the magistrate should be free and sitting in court while two innocent men were detained in custody and refused bail. McDonald would not let the verdict rest, and immediately took steps to try William Connelly for perjury. This time he searched high and low and, remarkably, found many new witnesses.

The most significant new witness was Mrs Maria Pearce. She said she saw Bourke and Connelly come out of Ayer's Hotel arm in arm, Connelly then dragged Bourke, who was drunk, against his will in the direction of McLaughlin's shed. Bourke fell down and Connelly struck him several times with a bottle. She did not come forward before because she thought Andersen and Hallinen, whom she knew to be innocent men, would get off and she did not wish to get mixed up in the affair. She now considered it her duty to come forward and give evidence.

As I read this I was relieved that finally someone had actually seen something, and that some concrete evidence had come to light. That is, until I read the next day's report in the paper ripping her statement to shreds on account of her alcoholism. There was some debate as to whether she could actually see that far from where she was standing, and I was amused to see she had appeared in court recently trying to obtain a divorce from her husband on the grounds that he was always drunk. This was also his claim against her.

However, slightly more credible was the statement from Mrs Johanna Phillips, a widow and a member of the Salvation Army for 20 years. She stated that she saw the two men coming from Price's corner to the shed, and she saw Mrs Maria Pearce standing in the street. She heard someone fall and then heard a deep groan. She had not told her story before as she had bad health, at times prone to fainting fits and did not think she could get through the trial.

It seemed that only now, when two innocent men had been sentenced to imprisonment, were the Westport locals willing to come forward and offer their help. I read a statement from the gaoler that seemed to sum up the town's feeling during the whole case. He said that at the beginning he, like everyone else, believed them to be guilty, but was convinced from their demeanour in gaol and from other information that they were innocent men, and that Connelly should have been arrested.

I began to see how the people of Westport were becoming involved in the case. It was while I was reading articles about the perjury trial that I spotted the first news of Andersen's decline in health. Despite the fact that things were looking up for the Norwegian, he collapsed in court with an epileptic seizure and had to be carried out. The article mentioned that his fits had come on since the start of the murder trial.

William Connelly, the actual murderer?
CANTERBURY TIMES, 26 MAY 1909, COURTESY CANTERBURY PUBLIC LIBRARY

The new evidence in Connelly's perjury trial gave Andersen and Hallinen alibis during the period the murder was supposed to have taken place, and clearly proved Connelly had made false statements.

McDonald's hard work paid off, and on 29 September Connelly was found guilty of eight counts of perjury during the previous trial, and now faced seven years' hard labour. He was read his sentence, and as he was escorted from the court, Detective McIlveney took it upon himself to interview Connelly about any other lies he may have told. He gained permission from the gaoler to talk to Connelly in the corridor of the court building at Hokitika before his removal to gaol. Connelly reportedly now confessed, "I alone killed Bourke. I knocked him down with my fist, and when he would not allow me to search him I lost my temper and kicked him in the face."

It was only a matter of days after Andersen's name was fully cleared that his condition worsened. Bed-ridden by epilepsy, he had been nursed at the Temperance Hotel in Westport during the later part of the trial. On 14 October 1908, he died. The papers reported his death was partly due to the worry and mental pain caused by his wrongful conviction. It seemed Anders had died of a broken heart.

After Connelly's confession, the seamen were pardoned, yet no compensation was offered, and the papers challenged the people of Westport to speak out against the injustice and ensure Connelly was tried for his self-confessed killing. On top of their feelings of responsibility for making the sailors suffer so long unnecessarily, they now had the death of Anders to compound their guilt.

A whole year after Bourke's death, the murderer, Connelly, was finally tried for the crime and found guilty. His sentence took his term of imprisonment up to 10 years. Poor Maria Pearce was called to the stand but was too drunk to give evidence on any of the days of the trial. The book about Hanlon had included a rather cruel cartoon about her in her inebriated state. Of all the books about the case, this one highlights Connelly's side. And I must admit it does provoke me to cast doubt on Andersen and Hallinen's story. I discovered Andersen never took the stand, on advice from McDonald, due to a previous conviction. He had earlier faced a charge of assault with intent to commit serious bodily harm and received three years. This was not the Anders I had envisioned!

I began to wonder if it was the wrongful accusation that was causing Anders so much grief — or was it the guilt of being the one actually responsible for the crime? But in the end, Connelly did confess to the crime, though to add another doubt to the story, he never confessed in court. His confession was instead drawn out of him in a court corridor after he had just been sentenced to seven years. What we can conclude is that the motive for the crime was robbery; and, indeed, Bourke's pipe was found on Connelly. If the seamen had been demanding money from Bourke in return for substantial quantities of tobacco, then why did no one report buying any from him?

The trial of William Connelly. CANTERBURY TIMES, 26 MAY 1909, COURTESY CANTERBURY PUBLIC LIBRARY

So, in the end I must agree the right man was found guilty. When Connelly committed the crime, though, I'm sure it wasn't his intention to kill. After he served his 10 years he would have been 28. What happened to him after that I couldn't find out.

When I visited Westport and wandered down Palmerston Street, I could visualise the action that would have gone on between all the different pubs on that cool May evening. Some of the buildings are still standing, including the old Westport Court, which is now a law office. I stood by Anders' grave and imagined the funeral service, attended by the guilt-ridden Westport locals.

With today's insight, I can't help but think that Anders could have been spared all his heartache if the technology of blood testing had been around, to prove straight away that Bourke's blood was nowhere near him. They did test the men's jackets and proved that the blood-like substance was blood, but that was as far as they could take it. In today's world my friend the forensic scientist, Dr Koelmeyer, could have solved this one in an instant.

The people of Westport never forgot poor Anders, whose heart was supposedly broken under the strain of wrongful accusations. Olaf Hallinen I presume sailed back to his homeland, as I could find no further trace of him. I was glossing over some of the earlier articles at the end of my readings about the trial when I found a description of Anders' physical features which included his tattoos. I really felt pity for this tragic figure when I read that Anders had a tattoo on his chest — over his broken heart — that said, "True Love".

T̄e Rongopai a Ruka/The Gospel of St Luke

As I STOOD ON the rise looking across the flat plains of the Waikato township of Waharoa, and on to the hills of the Kaimai Ranges beyond, I contemplated the tragedy at the heart of the story I was pursuing. Before me in an old urupa lay the gravesite of Tarore, a girl of just 12 years when she died a sudden and violent death in 1836. Lying amid unmarked graves, Tarore's last resting place has a gleaming white cross, with a matching picket fence.

Considering the long period of time since her death, Tarore's grave is well cared for. Not one but two inscriptions adorn her wooden cross. The one at the front contains a few scant details of her life; but most of the events with which she is now associated actually happened after her death. In fact, it is in her death rather than her life that she had achieved her notability.

143

EPITAPH

TARORE
AGED 12 YEARS
WHOSE MAORI GOSPEL OF ST LUKE
BROUGHT PEACE TO THE TRIBES OF AOTEAROA.
THE DAUGHTER OF NGAKUKU OF OKAVIA AND
GREAT NIECE OF TE WAHAROA OF MATAMATA.
SHE DIED AT WAIRERE FALLS ON 19TH OCTOBER 1836

At the back of the cross is another inscription that gives an introduction to the other characters that have played a large part in Tarore's afterlife:

TARORE, AGED 12 YEARS
THIS MEMORIAL WAS ERECTED BY THE BIBLE SOCIETY IN NEW ZEALAND AND
THE ELIAS TRUST AND C.M.S.
UNVEILED BY TE ARIKI NUI O NGA TANGATA MAORI,
NO NGA PENEI HOKI TE RANGATIRATANGA O TE ATUA.
TE RONGOPAI KI TE RITENGA A RUKA 18:16
16 OCT 1911

Why was the grave of such a young woman remembered in such a way, and by Maori and Pakeha alike? How could her Gospel bring peace?

The story of Tarore's life is in many ways the story of the people around her: her father Ngakuku, who converted to Christianity and worked alongside the missionary Alfred Brown; his uncle Te Waharoa, the paramount Ngati Haua rangatira after whom the township close by is named; her cousin and Te Waharoa's son Wiremu Tamihana Tarapipipi, who became known as 'The Kingmaker'; and the missionaries Alfred and Charlotte Brown.

Tarore's story led me into a fascinating period in our history, a time of great change, when Maori and Pakeha were involved in their first encounters. It was also a turbulent era for Maori, with intertribal skirmishes accelerating with the introduction of the musket; a time before the Treaty of Waitangi, when traders and missionaries were the first Pakeha contact with Maori settlements, and before the pressure for land acquisition for Pakeha settlement or the Land Wars had begun.

I started my sleuthing by checking out the list of names on Tarore's cross: the Bible Society in New Zealand, the Elias Trust and the CMS. The latter stood for the Church Missionary Society, which had recruited the missionary Brown to set up a mission in Matamata, where Tarore and her family lived. The "Elias" Trust turned out to be a spelling mistake for the "Elms Trust", which administered what had once been Alfred Brown's Tauranga mission site, which he established after he left Matamata.

On phoning the Bible Society, I was put through to a Gavin Drew, who the receptionist said had been involved with the Tarore story. What an understatement! Gavin talked so fast and with so much information that it was hard to get it all down. They had extensive information, much of it researched by a woman called Kathleen Holmes-Libbis, and now kept with their historian Dr Peter Lineham, who is a senior lecturer in history at Massey University. It was Kathleen Holmes-Libbis who had located the site of the grave and in so doing, discovered a cooking pot nearby, which dated from Tarore's time.

Sadly, Kathleen died some time ago, so I couldn't check out any details with her. However, there were many others who had followed her leads and who had adopted the story for themselves. Gavin had a lot to say about the telling of the story and its interpretation; for it has often been used as a parable rather than a historical account. Indeed, in many ways, it can be seen to represent the power of the word of God, the act of Christian forgiveness and the history of Maori evangelism in the 1800s. What follows is the closest to a verified version that I could ascertain from the research notes I was given and from the other enthusiasts I encountered during my search.

Alfred Brown. COURTESY THE ELMS TRUST, TAURANGA

IN 1835, TE WAHAROA, the paramount Ngati Haua rangatira, invited Alfred and Charlotte Brown to open a mission station at Matamata Pa. Although Te Waharoa himself never converted to Christianity, he allowed his people to take religious instruction from the Browns and offered them his protection both at Matamata Pa and later in Tauranga. Te Waharoa's second son, Tarapipipi, attended the Matamata Mission School and became a Christian convert.

Te Waharoa's nephew, Ngakuku, was from Ngati Haua and a rangatira of Okauia Pa. He joined Brown's mission station, becoming a convert and one of Brown's religious workers. His wife was dead but he had two children: a daughter Tarore; and a younger son. Ngakuku encouraged the religious instruction of Tarore, who was taught by Charlotte or "Mother" Brown in her girls' section of the Mission School. Here she learnt to read and write in Maori and was given biblical instruction from *Te Rongopai a Ruka/The Gospel of St Luke*. Tarore apparently had a copy of her father's *Te Rongopai a Ruka* on which his name was said to be inscribed. She carried this everywhere in a kete or pouch that she wore around her neck.

During the 1830s, there were many ongoing battles between the Waikato tribes and Te Arawa from Rotorua. This was the time of utu or retribution, when killing repaid killing. In December 1835, Te Hunga, a relation of Te Waharoa, was killed by Te Arawa. In utu, a combined taua or war party attacked Te Arawa at Maketu on 28 March 1836. Te Arawa retaliated on 5 May by destroying Ngai Te Rangi's Pa at Te Tumu. In August, Te Waharoa with Ngati Haua attacked Ngati Whakaue at Ohinemutu. Thomas Chapman's mission station there was caught in the crossfire and destroyed, but Tarapipipi (Te Waharoa's son) and one of Brown's converts managed to lead the missionaries to safety.

Brown visited the destroyed mission, and, as Te Waharoa could no longer guarantee the Matamata mission protection, Brown decided to move to Te Papa, in Tauranga, now home of "The Elms". This was the catalyst for the ensuing tragedy.

An advance party set out from the mission station at Matamata, carrying an

The Wairere Waterfall, just above the site of the group's camp. GREENSTONE PICTURES

assortment of the mission goods and the Browns' furniture. Among them was Ngakuku together with Tarore, her younger brother, many of the mission station children and John Flatt, an agricultural assistant. The journey took them over the long and steep Wairere Falls Track, which traverses the Kaimai Ranges and was the main thoroughfare for Maori and Pakeha travellers at that time. It was an important link to Tauranga and the coast, used in trade, exploration, warfare and missionary expeditions alike. Today the Wairere Falls Track is well maintained and very beautiful: interestingly shaped boulders and rocks give way to bush and light-filtered treescapes. The walk would have been a pleasant, though steep, one.

The group camped for the night at a resting place on the Wairere Track. Flatt had erected a tent and the others slept in an existing raupo hut built for travellers. I could imagine, as there were so few adults with them and no armed guards, that the party was not expecting any trouble on what must have been a routine trip which many would have done numerous times before. The night scenes were likely to have been happy, filled with the things that children do, even though they were tired. But the sense of happy adventure was not to last.

In the middle of the night, the camp dogs began to bark. The smoke from the fires must have been seen by a small Te Arawa taua, for chaos ensued. There would have been great confusion, petrified screams, fear — everyone rushing about in the semi-darkness, and all getting away to safety among the trees — all except Tarore. I could feel Ngakuku's panic — helping his young son to escape, probably thinking his elder daughter would be able to make good her own escape — running, fleeing until at a safe distance, trying to find everyone . . . then the awful realisation that Tarore was not with them.

The stories of her death give gruesome detail of the top of her skull and her heart being removed and taken. Her precious Gospel was also taken.

Flatt remained in his tent but was not killed; however, some of his clothes and possessions were taken, including his breeches. He later rode off on his horse to Tauranga wearing only the shirt he had been left. In his accounts of the attack, he seems more indignant at the robbery of his clothing than at Tarore's murder.

At about 7 am, some youths from Tarore's mission party reached Brown back in Matamata in a disturbed state and told him of the attack. About two hours later, after what must have been a heartbreaking journey, the distraught Ngakuku arrived carrying the body of his daughter. He begged Brown to give Tarore a Christian burial and was said to be distressed as to whether she would go to "Heaven or to Te Reinga". The anger, horror and despair he must have felt would have been unbearable.

On the 20 October, Tarore was buried at Matamata Pa with a Christian service. Her name could have been buried amid further acts of retribution — she was, after all, the grand-niece of the paramount chief — but her father turned the tide of war and of history by his address at the funeral, recorded by Brown:

> There lies my child. She has been murdered as a payment for your bad conduct, but do not rise to seek payment for her. God will do that. Let this be the finishing of the war with Rotorua. Now let peace be made. My heart is not dark for Tarore but for you. You urged teachers to come to you — they came — and now you are driving them away. You

are crying for my girl. I am crying for you, for myself, for all of us. Perhaps this is a sign of God's anger towards us for our sins. Turn to him. Believe or else you will all perish.

Through Ngakuku's words, Tarore's memory was to live on, though I was to find that her Gospel, pulled from the pouch at her neck, was to take the story further yet.

Apparently, Tarore's copy of *Te Rongopai a Ruka/The Gospel of St Luke* was taken back to Te Arawa, where Uira or Uita, who some versions say was in the taua party that attacked Tarore, had taken it. Uita was said to have been unable to read, but a man called Ripahau, who was from Otaki and returning to his people after being released from enslavement up north, stayed at Uita's pa. Coming from the north, which was then a missionary stronghold, Ripahau had been taught to read, so he read Tarore's Gospel aloud to Uita. It is believed that when Uita heard the words, he repented and some years later when he met Ngakuku asked for his forgiveness for Tarore's killing and was granted it.

Ripahau was reported to have taken the Gospel back to Kapiti Island to Te Rauparaha's son, who had been baptised Wiremu Tamehana Te Rauparaha (also known as Katu) and his cousin Matene Te Whiwhi. Katu Te Rauparaha and Matene Te Whiwhi then in turn took it around the South Island preaching to both their own Ngati Toa relations and the Southern tribes that their father and uncle Te Rauparaha had previously attacked.

Although the suggestion that Tarore's actual Gospel was taken on the evangelical trail

Tarapipipi the Kingmaker. JOHN KINDER ALBUM, 1863: B8430. AUCKLAND WAR MEMORIAL MUSEUM

is disputed, Peter Lineham believes the whole story is well authenticated by a number of sources.

What happened to the others in Tarore's story? On Good Friday 1839, Ngakuku was baptised by Brown with the name Wiremu Maihi (William Marsh). Before this time, and for many years after, he travelled to various places — such as Opotiki, Tolaga Bay, East Coast — evangelising and teaching with Brown and his fellow CMS workers.

Te Waharoa died in 1838, and his second son Tarapipipi succeeded his father as rangatira. In 1839, Tarapipipi was baptised with the name Wiremu Tamehana or William Thompson by Brown at his Tauranga mission. Tarapipipi was to continue a long relationship both with Brown and with Christianity, and set up his own Christian pa in the Matamata area: Te Tapiri in 1839, and Peria in 1846. For many years he tried to bring peace into the Waikato, often petitioning and negotiating with the government to stop the tide of settlement and land acquisition. He became known as 'The Kingmaker' for his role in persuading Potatau to become the first Maori King. At the coronation, Tarapipipi held the Bible above the head of the new monarch, a role that has been continued by his descendants, just as the name "Kingmaker" has been passed on.

So, Tarore's murder had enormous repercussions for many people. But what of Tarore herself? Her story has become a

The Tauranga mission as it stands today (above) and the chapel as it was when first built (below).
ABOVE: GREENSTONE PICTURES. BELOW: JOHN KINDER ALBUM B966, AUCKLAND WAR MEMORIAL MUSEUM

The Matamata whare (above) and the girls' school (left). LEFT: KINDER ALBUM C1748; ABOVE: B8251, AUCKLAND WAR MEMORIAL MUSEUM

powerful symbol, but I had little sense of her as a real person. As a father, myself, I felt great sympathy for Ngakuku and I wanted to get a picture of the girl. I therefore visited The Elms, hoping to find something more of her. She had been close to the Browns and their teachings, and perhaps I could pick up, at the mission house, a sense of where they were moving when the tragedy occurred.

It appears that the Browns and their party lived in raupo whare from the time they first moved to Tauranga in 1838 until 1847, when the mission house was finished. The spot where the whare once stood is marked now by a stone cairn. Sadly, the Browns were to endure a similar loss to Ngakuku's. They also had two children, a daughter, Celia, and a son, Marsh, who was to die in 1945, aged 14, after a long illness. He was about the same age as Tarore's brother and had the same name as Ngakuku adopted on baptism. I couldn't help but surmise that the families were very close and would have keenly mourned each other's losses.

Although the mission house was built after Tarore's death, it does give a feeling for the times, reflecting the missionary aspiration to live like English gentry. It is generously proportioned with large, shuttered windows, and a separate building to house the library. It contains numerous artefacts belonging to the Browns, including journals, clothing, Brown's bowler hats adorned with archdeacon rosettes (although he was not made an archdeacon until about 1842). The house also contains original oil portraits of Alfred, Charlotte and their daughter Celia, as well as watercolours of the grounds and a raupo whare similar to the one that the Browns lived in when they first moved there. As I had been unable to verify what the Matamata mission station looked like, I assumed that because of the limited time the Browns were there, it too may have been a raupo whare. I searched for the cooking pot found at Tarore's grave and said to be kept at the mission house, but could find only a forgotten old pot that looked far too big.

I was getting close to the end of my journey to learn about Tarore, but I still wondered what she looked like. During a final trip to the Auckland War Memorial Museum Library, I checked the catalogue for John Kinder's early photographs. He married Alfred and Charlotte Brown's daughter Celia, and was a prolific photographer and artist of the period. The library has three volumes of his photos — many taken of Church properties around the country. Some photos in volume three particularly drew my attention. One of them has the inscription: "Large Native House, Te Wai o Turongo House, Matamata". I assumed that this was the old Matamata, the pa that is now in Waharoa and where Tarore had lived. Perhaps these people photographed, particularly the old man, knew Tarore, Ngakuku and Brown.

There are also photos taken of Te Papa, Tauranga (The Elms) showing Brown's mission house and chapel. One of them is significant even if it is taken some 30 years after Tarore's death; it shows "Native Girls' School, Te Papa, Tauranga, 1862". Half a dozen young Maori girls stand at the door, looking at the camera. They are a visual indication of how Tarore may have looked, and I felt that I was now in touch with the person behind the story as well as the parable it lead to. By the girls' feet is a pile of huge cooking pots, very like the one I had found at The Elms, so perhaps that was the correct pot I'd found after all. While I didn't discover what that pot signified, for me it conjures up another image of Tarore, for after her mother's death it would have fallen to her to prepare her family's meals. I could picture her small figure tending the fires and caring for her father and small brother.

I returned from the museum to find in the mail an article about Tarore's relation and namesake, Tarore Lorraine Emson. I tracked down Tarore Lorraine who had her own family stories of Tarore, including one about the pouch that held the Gospel. It was retrieved after the murder and buried with one of Tarore Lorraine's ancestors. The current Tarore is bright and cheerful with shining eyes and a positive attitude. She is a tangible and living link to Tarore the young girl. Seeing her, I now found it easy to imagine Tarore as a vibrant, beautiful girl, and I felt again Ngakuku's huge loss. My lasting feeling is one of awe at his amazing strength to offer forgiveness and call for peace.

Somebody's Darling

CROSSING THE MILLER'S FLAT bridge that spans the Clutha, I spotted a signpost; on one of its enamel-yellow fingers is written "LONELY GRAVES 9 km". Following that sign along the river, I came to a white picket fence alongside the road enclosing two graves. The graves and the road are the only evidence of human life you can see for miles around. It is lonely . . . most of the time. But despite the remoteness, these graves are visited by hundreds of people each year. They aren't relatives; in fact, the two men buried here are not known to have any relatives in New Zealand. They, like thousands of others in the middle of last century, came to this country alone, hoping to become rich, mainly from the gold that was being dug out of Otago. I suppose they were the beginning of a culture of men working alone against the land.

The two men lying in the graves never met when they were alive. It is only in death they have become inseparable, buried together in this remote spot. One grave has two headstones; the original wooden one erected in 1865 reads:

SOMEBODY DARLING LIES BURIED HERE

At first I thought the engraver had made a grammatical mistake, but if you look closely you can still make out the apostrophe S after the word "Somebody". The marble headstone that was erected later has the same message with the word "Somebody's" clearly legible. And next to these stones is another headstone with a related message. It reads:

WILLIAM RIGNEY
THE MAN WHO BURIED SOMEBODY'S DARLING

152

So many people have sent me letters about the Lonely Graves I think they must be the best-known burial sites in New Zealand. Most of those writing seemed to know the story behind these rather cryptic headstones. It's this story, and the amazing setting, that attract people to this tiny cemetery.

William Rigney came to New Zealand in 1861. He was an Irishman, born in Loughrea, County Galway in 1833. After being expelled from a theological seminary in Ireland, he made his way to Australia, where he worked as a tutor. He came on to New Zealand following the news of a goldstrike that drew men from all over the world to the Otago goldfields. He went directly to Gabriel's Gully where the great goldrush began and followed new strikes, arriving in Horseshoe Bend near Miller's Flat in 1865. And there he stayed. For the next 47 years nothing much happened in Horseshoe Bend that Rigney didn't know about.

He was well-educated and evidently verbally sharp as befitting someone who had spent most of their life at loggerheads with authority. Although difficult, he was a hard worker and his concern for others linked him forever to the grave of Somebody's Darling.

As the story goes, one day, when Rigney had gone down to the river to see if flood waters had receded enough to continue work on his claim, he found the body of a young man washed up on the river's edge. Such a find was not uncommon. Between February 1864 and March 1865, 28 people had drowned in the goldfield district. Many of them were known only by a Christian name or a nickname, and their families would have

Early miners lived a rough life in remote, untamed areas. ALEXANDER TURNBULL LIBRARY F117280 1/2

been untraceable. Four of them were never identified — the death records list them simply as "person name unknown". Such was the fate of the man found by Rigney. After an inquest had failed to identify the body, it was destined to be buried in an unmarked grave.

The thought of someone dying in a strange land without even a name on their tombstone obviously touched Rigney deeply; the dead man was, after all, somebody's son, brother or sweetheart — somebody's darling. Following the inquest, Rigney was said to have buried the young man at the now-famous spot, carving a headstone with the famous inscription and tending the grave for many years.

As time passed, the inscription began to fade. It appears someone less literary than Rigney wrote over the original text with a hot poker and omitted the apostrophe and S. In 1903, in recognition of the grave's sentimental place in local history, it was decided to erect a more permanent headstone made of marble. The old headstone was discarded and then rediscovered many years later in a nearby gully. It was then placed in a glass case where it can be viewed at the foot of the marble stone. The new stone is a more lasting memorial but it has nothing of the rough tenderness of the wooden slab.

Despite the biting wind of a Southland winter, I was pleased to have come to this place and seen it for myself. It is a great story. Out here in the middle of nowhere, this monument is a reminder of compassion in a time when life was hard. In the physically and emotionally tough environment of the goldfields, Rigney's kindness must have touched people, and it still does.

I retreated to my car and thermos of tea. It is bitter in these parts. What must it have been like for the men who lived here in frustrated squalor, dreaming of striking it rich and most of them just wasting years and drifting away or dying, anonymously? Thousands of families would have said farewell to husbands and sons and then never heard of them again.

I returned to Miller's Flat because the local storekeeper there is a keen historian and has a lot of old papers and photographs. There's only one general store in the town, so I knew Betty Adams wouldn't be hard to find. Many of the visitors to the Lonely Graves come past her store, and she is happy to tell them the story of William Rigney. It has been written up in many books on Southland's history and is part of the local folklore. It's the story people want to hear.

Perhaps this is the reason Betty Adams doesn't also tell the visitors to read a little book that's actually for sale in the shop. It's called *One Man's Goldfield* and says the story of the Lonely Graves is a myth. Such a claim might be dismissable if it weren't for a letter that Betty showed me. It was written by William Rigney himself in 1901 and addressed to the editor of the *Tuapeka Times* in response to an item that had appeared in the newspaper.

> Sir — as there were one or two slight mistakes in Saturday's issue regarding the Lonely Graves at Horseshoe Bend I thought I'd send you a few lines stating the real facts of the case. The body which is buried there was found on a beach on the West side of the river opposite Horseshoe Bend in the early days. I don't know the time but it was before I came to the locality in 1865.

Rigney's siding at Miller's Flat still bears the name of the man "who buried" Somebody's Darling.

By his own admission, William Rigney didn't bury Somebody's Darling! The letter goes on:

> There was nothing done to enclose the grave until a man named John Ord and myself put a fence of rough manuka round it. I had to go to Tapanui for mining timbers and I got a board of black pine. This I shaped into something like a headstone, painted it white, and with a tomahawk and a four inch nail I cut, or rather sank into the timber the words "Somebody's Darling Lies Buried Here".

So, despite the official histories and the longevity of the legend, Rigney didn't find or bury the body at all, though Rigney is responsible for the famous epitaph. I decided to go to the Hocken Library to look through the old newspapers. This was when I discovered a further twist to the folklore — when he died, people knew who Somebody's Darling was!

A report on the inquest into the drowning was published in the paper. According to this, the inquest was held at the Horse Shoe Hotel on the 22 February 1865. A miner named Robert Harrison said that on 7 February he found the body lying face down in the sand at Rag Beach on Horseshoe Bend. A description of the clothing coincided with evidence given by a ferryman from Teviot who had heard about the drowning and knew the deceased because he frequently crossed the river on the Dunstan Ferry.

The *Otago Daily Times* published an article which said that on Wednesday 25 January 1865 a 25-year-old butcher from Nevis called Charles Alms was drowned trying to swim cattle across the river at Muttontown Creek, near Clyde. All the facts, the clothing, the general description of the man, the timing of his death and the location of the corpse at Rag Beach pointed to this being the body of Charles Alms.

Because the body was badly decomposed, no formal identification could be given. That meant, according to the law of the day, that no death certificate could be issued. Record of his death was limited to what was reported in the papers. No relatives were found.

So, according to the new version of the story, William Rigney arrived a few months after the body had been buried. I wondered how it was that if all the local people knew, despite official technicalities, that the body was Charles Alms's, why wasn't Rigney told of this, especially as the man who had helped him make the fence around the grave was a local schoolteacher? And if everyone knew who the dead man was, why did no one give him a headstone?

I found an explanation to this when I looked at a map of the region. Nevis, where Alms lived, is barely populated and is roughly 100 km by road northwest of Horseshoe Bend. Alms met his accident at Muttontown Creek, near Clyde, about 40 km from Nevis and 60 km from Horseshoe Bend. He may never have been further south than Alexandra. The ferryman lived in Teviot, a little way north of Horseshoe Bend, but may well have worked along various stretches of the river so, unlike those in Horseshoe Bend, he probably would have known a large number of people from all over the area. On the other hand, the few inhabitants of the tiny settlement of Horseshoe Bend would probably have headed south to Gore, Milton or Balclutha if they wanted to visit a larger township, rather than north to the smaller settlement of Clyde. So, it is very likely that

Alms was unknown to the people of Horseshoe Bend. Even today, the region is sparsely populated and surrounded by rugged mountains. In Alms's time, travel was by foot or horse, so it is reasonable to surmise that if he had close friends in Nevis or Clyde, they would not necessarily have known about the inquest at Horseshoe Bend; or if they did, would not have been able to make the long trip to Alms' final resting place. The locals at Horseshoe Bend may have had a possible name for the corpse that had travelled so far down the river, but he was, in all probability, a complete stranger.

But why was Rigney touched to act as a friend to a man he never met? Perhaps an answer is contained in Rigney's letter to the editor of the *Tuapeka Times*.

> I have always felt a special interest in that grave as I have a foreboding that in the end my lot will be the same — a lonely grave on a bleak hillside.

This proved to be a very prophetic observation. Maybe because of his quarrelsome habits, or as a hangover from his early years in the priesthood, or just the roughness of mining life, Rigney never married or had any children. I don't know whether it was at his request that when he died he was buried next to the grave of Somebody's Darling. Perhaps, despite all his protests to the contrary, local legend had inextricably bound Rigney to the Lonely Grave at Horseshoe Bend.

Certainly, the tale of how Rigney had found and buried the young man has stuck so fast that most people don't know it any differently. Despite the fact that Rigney didn't bury Somebody's Darling and that this man was in all likelihood called Charles Alms, the folklore persists. In the end, even the truth doesn't stand in the way of a good story.

People continue to visit the two Lonely Graves. Rigney gave the unmarked burial site dignity and showed kindness and respect for a stranger. His compassion is the lasting memory of this remote spot. This, after all, is what Rigney is really remembered for; and perhaps so many are drawn here because we all carry the same hope that we, too, will be remembered as somebody's darling.

gainst the Elements

THE RE ARE NUMEROUS EPITAPHS that are the only remaining sign of a life that, once extinguished, is virtually untraceable. It is a growing obsession of many to try and rekindle these flames. We are fascinated with the archeology of time, the layers of history and the details of lives lived. It probably has a lot to do with our own fear of transience, the fear that we, like all these others, might leave nothing that marks our own passage. But occasionally I find a memorial to someone whose life shed a light so strong it is still visible, someone whose talent and vision remains.

In the Dunedin North Cemetery there is a large gravestone bearing a Celtic cross, its lines filled in with bold stone flowers, and standing on either side of the stone are large stone lighthouses. The inscription reads:

IN MEMORY OF
JAMES MELVILLE BALFOUR
COLONIAL MARINE ENGINEER
WHO DROWNED OFF TIMARU
ON THE 18TH DECEMBER 1869
AGED 38 YEARS

ALSO OF HIS WIFE CHRISTINA SIMSON
WHO DIED AT SAINT SERVAN FRANCE
ON 30TH APRIL 1897
AGED 60 YEARS

RE-UNITED

Next to this is an even taller headstone, also crowned with a beautiful Celtic cross. Its inscription reads:

THOMAS PATERSON M.I.G.E.
BORN AT EDINBURGH
25TH DECEMBER 1830
DROWNED WHEN CROSSING THE KAKANUI RIVER
15TH DECEMBER 1869

TO THE DEAR MEMORY OF A DUTIFUL SON
AND DEVOTED BROTHER
HIS AGED FATHER ERECTS THIS STONE

The two men died within days of each other. They are buried in plots that adjoin each other. I was to discover that this was no coincidence, for here lay a story of lifelong companionship, of brilliance, zeal and the hand of destiny.

Searching in an Otago library, I found several books that looked promising sources of information — for example, *Early New Zealand Engineers* and *The Lighthouses of New Zealand*. Sure enough, there they were: James Balfour and Thomas Paterson. In *Marine Department: Centennial History*, the foreword begins

When James Balfour, a brilliant young engineer, forsook his native Scotland in 1863 for the rigours of early life in this country he would not realise the part he was destined to play in the early history of New Zealand.

James and Thomas were both born in Edinburgh and grew up there together. By the time they finished high school, the two men had decided on their careers. Thomas was to be a road and rail engineer and went to train under a railway contractor, and would soon become the company's

James Balfour. FROM F.W. FURKERT, EARLY NEW ZEALAND ENGINEERS, COURTESY REED PUBLISHING

managing assistant. James's path was almost predetermined. Born into the illustrious Stevenson family, who were renowned lighthouse builders and engineers, James was always going to follow the family tradition (unlike his nephew Robert Louis Stevenson, though both were to travel to the southern hemisphere). After studying marine engineering in Scotland and Germany, it was natural for him to join the family firm.

A career in engineering in the nineteenth century must be like a career in computing in the twentieth; engineers were opening up the world. They were conquering distance and speed and were the technical pioneers. Throughout the West, engineers were pushing roads and rail into hinterlands, they were carving harbours out of shorelines and were building great bridges across chasms and lighthouses on clifftops. In 1863, James Balfour and Thomas Paterson were offered the opportunity and challenge to use their skills to open up a young country in the antipodes.

The Otago Provincial Government, in an attempt to keep pace with the population boom, devised a policy to bring a first-class marine engineer and a first-class road engineer out to New Zealand. The government promised each a free passage and the handsome wage of 1000 pounds a year for two years, with a return passage if the officer didn't wish to remain. In response to the Provisional Government's request, Stevenson's Engineering of Scotland recommended the employment of James Balfour and Thomas Paterson.

Thomas was the first to arrive and was immediately appointed the Otago railway and road engineer. James arrived in September with his wife Christina Simson and daughter Marie. The two friends lived close to each other in the very centre of the city, Balfour in Princes Street and Paterson in Rattray Street, and they both had offices in Princes Street.

For James and Thomas, it must have been strange coming across the world to a city that was established to emulate directly the city they'd just come from. Dunedin is the Gaelic word for Edinburgh, and Edinburgh's street plan was used as a template by Dunedin city planners. Dunedin city residents were mostly Scottish immigrants, and everyone spoke with a pronounced Scottish accent. The bagpipes, the tartans, even a marked dislike for the English had been imported too.

But as yet, the city had nothing of the centuries-old beauty of Edinburgh. In the early 1860s, the streets of Dunedin

Shipwrecks were common in Balfour's day.
LA BELLA, ALEXANDER TURNBULL LIBRARY P56548 1/2

were still unpaved and construction was going on everywhere. The goldrush fever was passing, but Otago had garnered its share of the rewards. It was a prosperous city, the largest and fastest-growing in New Zealand at the time. According to meeting records and papers, everyone was complaining about the roads and transport. Enter James Balfour and Thomas Paterson.

Paterson had been in the country only a few days when he was called to give evidence on the comparative advantages of railways or roads to open up the country. The need for roads to provide access into and across the Otago Province was immediate, and initially this consumed Paterson's time. He was engaged in the construction of the two main roads to the goldfields — one via Lawrence and the other via The Pigroot — and was responsible for the abandonment of the hazardous central route via the Rock and Pillar ranges.

Balfour was likewise loaded with work that needed immediate attention. Within six months of his arrival, he had already prepared plans for the Dog Island and Tairoa Heads lighthouses and was busy working on a proposal for a lighthouse at Cape Saunders. It is fitting that Balfour's first achievement, the Tairoa lighthouse, to this day guides vessels into Dunedin.

There are piles of letters and reports written by James Balfour that lie in neat bundles in the Hocken Library in Dunedin. He was consulted on virtually everything to do with water, reservoirs, dams, breakwaters and graving docks (where ships were cleaned). He designed models to test his theories on shingle drift and harbour currents, and these have all been preserved. As well as writing commissioned reports, there are a number of other technical submissions Balfour made. For example, when he was surveying the Clutha River, he discovered the surface water speed was quite different from the water speed at depth. All this is well known now, but it was obviously new to Balfour and his colleagues. When he was assessing the site for the Farewell Spit lighthouse, he discovered there was an error in the Admiralty charts and he re-surveyed the coastline.

In October 1864, he chaired a commission on the development of Port Chalmers; three months later he was advising a sanitary commission in Dunedin. From there he put together proposals for harbours in New Plymouth, Timaru and Wanganui. In Wellington, Balfour was asked to advise on the best site for a bridge over the Hutt River. He also designed a graving dock for Wellington Harbour, and although it was never built, the design was so innovative the plans have been kept in the Wellington Museum. He also surveyed Cook Strait for the laying of a submarine cable. By November 1865, Balfour was at work on a new plan for dredging Otago Harbour.

The year 1865 was big for Dunedin. Fire tore through a block in Princes Street as far as Rattray Street and heralded the construction of large inner-city stone buildings to replace the wooden ones that had perished. Dunedin was beginning to take on the visual stature of its namesake. It was also the year of the Great Exhibition. Popular worldwide, these exhibitions were a great drawcard for tourists and money. James Balfour was involved in the engineering projects for the Great Exhibition and at the same time he was busy testing the properties of local timber, for a reason that became apparent when he took up office as marine engineer.

It was 1866 when James Balfour was appointed General Governor Marine Engineer for the colony of New Zealand. The appointment carried with it the additional title of

Superintendent of Lighthouses. This was, with hindsight, the genesis of the Marine Department.

Balfour now had a free hand with which to sketch plans for the colony's development. He reportedly went at the task with great passion and dedication. I've read descriptions of James Balfour as a mild-mannered, personable man. These descriptions are two-a-penny in history books. They seem to be stock phrases used to vouch for the character of someone who had no obvious faults and no peculiar personality traits. The comments I've read of Balfour in work reports probably describe him better. He was obviously a superb administrator and the accolades variously describe him as "a driving force" and "an eminent engineer". He obviously had a lot of concern for the human part played in the mechanics of modernisation, and lighthouse keepers came under his spotlight. At the time Balfour took office, there were only 15 lighthouse keepers in New Zealand, four of whom had been dismissed because of drunkenness or insubordination. What keepers seemed to be lacking was a clear brief of their responsibilities. The Calvinist tradition of

Balfour's lighthouse at Farewell Spit, built in 1870. ALEXANDER TURNBULL LIBRARY G986-10x8

morality for which the Scots were renowned was about to be imposed on those in the lighthouse service.

Balfour's edicts were that the principal keeper should gather all staff and family together every Sunday to conduct prayers. The men were to be always sober and their workplace and homes were to be clean and orderly. Where there were more than two keepers to a lighthouse, the men would take turns keeping watch, while in sole-keeper houses they were required to sleep in the lightroom. The lights had to be cleaned carefully and meticulously and the lenses themselves were only allowed to be polished with a feather duster and a chamois.

The laying down of rules extended on as Balfour compiled harbour and quarantine regulations for the colony, set down standards for the examination of masters and engineers of steamers, and introduced a general code of danger signals for the whole of the New Zealand coast.

James Balfour was always looking to improve on technology. It was he who ran tests to determine the efficiency of paraffin and then had all lighthouses in New Zealand adapted to burn paraffin instead of oil. Another potential limitation was that New Zealand's lighthouses had to be cast in steel in England and brought out in pieces by ship and assembled. Balfour wanted to build in a material readily available locally: wood. He undertook numerous experiments into the feasibility of using New Zealand hard timbers. Time was of the essence, and this was the fastest way to erect coastal lights around the country. Sea traffic was busy and the coastline treacherous; and up to the time of Balfour's appointment there had been 500 recorded shipwrecks around the coast. The first wooden lighthouse was completed at Farewell Spit in 1870, a lattice construction, 100 feet tall.

One of the many reports Balfour completed was a full appraisal of all New Zealand's lighthouses. This reveals a very good knowledge of many forms of engineering and optical principles, and up-to-date knowledge of advances in the science of optics elsewhere in the world. In the first few pages of the report, he praises the company of Stevenson's in Edinburgh at least half a dozen times, and at one point he justifies his emulation of the Scottish system, saying, "The Scottish lighthouses are stated in the Report of the last Commission of Investigation in 1861, to be the best in the Kingdom, and, as they also state British lights to be unsurpassed, by inference the best in the world."

Something that caught my eye as I was reading the lighthouse report was a reference Balfour made to Cape Saunders as "one of the most important sites for a lighthouse on the East Coast of the Middle Island". It was only in the very early days of the colony that what we now know as the South was called the Middle Island. Dunedin had been founded only 15 years earlier. I struggle to imagine just what life must have been like for these pioneers so early on.

Just one last note about my dippings into the *Marine Department: Centennial History*. A lighthouse keeper's annual wage varied between 110 and 250 pounds and the inspectors of steamers who worked out of Balfour's office were being paid 375 pounds a year. At 1000 pounds a year, Balfour was, at least, being justly rewarded.

Thomas Paterson raises his head in the history books again in 1864 when he resigned his position in charge of roads. The young engineer was so overburdened with work that he couldn't oversee this area and work on rail simultaneously. He was officially appointed Chief Engineer for Railways of the Province in April 1865. That same year he planned the rail route through the Taieri District, and in 1866 he was put in charge of the Winton–Invercargill Railway. He also designed the old bridge over the Clutha, now under Lake Dunstan at Cromwell. Thomas consulted on the Oreti Railway in Southland, built the Rakaia Bridge, worked for Canterbury Railway and reported on work to make the Lyttelton Tunnel safe.

James and Thomas remained close friends all this time. At one point they were working together, for in 1867 James gave evidence to a parliamentary committee on railway gauges, recommending that they adopt the cheap type and leave the cost of upgrading to posterity. Thomas was closely involved in the issue over the next two years. Our small gauge railway system remains today.

By 1869 James Balfour was living in Wellington. That year he wrote a prophetic report to the government outlining the dangers to the public he had found during the course of his employment in New Zealand, generally the lack of bridges, forcing people "to cross dangerous fords", and the want of harbours, "forcing people to embark and disembark by means of surfboats".

In making these two points, Balfour unknowingly prophesied the circumstances of two impending deaths. One of these would be Paterson's. His death was just one of more than 1100 recorded drownings in New Zealand rivers alone by 1870. Drownings were so common that in some graveyards, the rivers and the sea account for more lives lost than all other deaths combined.

It was late in 1869, and Balfour was in Timaru overseeing the construction of an experimental breakwater. Like so many of his designs, this concept was new to New Zealand. The breakwater was to be made of cement sited on a shallow reef. The concrete base for the breakwater had to be built between tides, and the first attempt was thwarted, not by rising water but by rising wages. The labourers wanted a pay rise and stopped work halfway through the job. The tide came in and washed the unfinished block away. Two days later, another attempt was made and, despite a heavy sea, the new block, covered with tarpaulins and weighed down with tons of old cable, stood firm. Work had been in progress for two weeks, with Balfour staying on in Timaru, when he received news of Thomas Paterson's death.

Thomas was returning to Dunedin on the Cobb & Co Coach Service with his plans for the Rangitata Bridge. There had been heavy rain, but the coach driver completed the first ford of the swollen Kakanui River without any trouble. However, when water started to fill the coach at the second ford, the driver turned back. Broadside to the current, the coach and horses were dragged 50 metres downstream. The lead horses made the bank, but at this point the coach wrenched free and was swept away.

The Cobb & Co Coach making one of its many river crossings. AUCKLAND CITY LIBRARIES A10082

Surfboats were used to carry passengers to and from ships anchored beyond the breakers.
ALEXANDER TURNBULL LIBRARY G4953 1/1

Remarkably, when the coach was washed ashore only two passengers were unaccounted for — a local schoolteacher and Thomas Paterson. The next day, Thomas's body was found pinned under the coach.

Balfour was determined to make it back to Dunedin for the funeral on 19 December. The *Maori*, a trade steamer, was at anchor in the harbour channel bound for Dunedin. There was a nasty easterly swell running and the ship's cargo couldn't be unloaded, but Balfour and the other passengers decided to go aboard. A surfboat set out, but in the harbour it fouled a buoy and a lifeboat had to be launched from the steamer. The passengers were transferred from boat to boat successfully and all was well until the lifeboat drew in alongside the *Maori*. The crest of a wave suddenly capsized the lifeboat. Lines and lifebuoys were thrown to the passengers and one by one they were hauled on board. By the time the line reached James, he was too exhausted to hold on to it and drowned. His body was recovered from the beach several days later.

The rivers that Paterson worked to bridge claimed his life. The harbours Balfour worked to make safe claimed his life. It seems fatefully tragic that these men were claimed by the forces they were determined to conquer.

The Taieri Gorge Railway is a striking monument to the talents of Thomas Paterson. It is now a major tourist attraction, and when I took the trip I found it quite awe-inspiring. Paterson's ability to defy nature and tame the landscape amazed me, and similarly Balfour's lighthouses are testament to his drive to conquer the natural elements — to deprive them of their power to take human life. These two men met the forces of nature head-on in a contest that ultimately nature would win but not before they had achieved in six years what many would dream of achieving in a lifetime. Their deaths were a terrible loss to this young country; however, like the light from Nugget Point Lighthouse that still radiates its brilliance out to sea, the lights of Thomas Paterson's and James Balfour's endeavours still shine just as brightly.

Researching History's Mysteries

Making the television series *Epitaph* involved many hours of detailed research by a team of experienced researchers. For my own part I was very much a novice to begin with, but as with most things the more you do, the easier it gets. I discovered that much of the information usually comes relatively easily, but getting those extra details that bring you closer to the people and the story and provide valuable insights can be much more painstaking but very rewarding. For example, in the case of Hugh Hamilton, because someone took the trouble to go through the *Police Gazette*, we discovered the loss of Hugh's pet canary. This was a trivial incident in itself but in the context of Hugh's domestic situation, it assumed much more importance. Similarly, in the story of Winiata, because someone was prepared to pore through great tracts of Hansard, we were rewarded with the knowledge that Winiata's capture had huge political significance and that the government was probably behind it. Being a commercial operation, time was our greatest enemy. Research takes time, but if you have it, then research can be great fun and, I have to warn you, very addictive. The following is by no means a comprehensive guide. It's more of a starter kit for the enthusiastic beginner.

Family history

There is a rapidly growing number of people interested in tracing their roots, as evidenced by the establishment of the Family Research Centre at Auckland Central City Library. As well as their excellent resources, there are also many different guides and "how to" books.

- Start with what you know and begin a basic family tree.

- Talk to relatives and old family friends for names. Collect together any papers and photos that might be in the family.

- Use the Births, Deaths and Marriages Indexes on microfiche. These provide the names of all the people who were born, died or married in New Zealand and are catalogued by the year. They can be found at genealogy centres, libraries and Latter Day Saints (Mormon) family history centres. This index gives you a reference number, which you can quote at the Registry office to acquire the certificate.

- Send for copies of these certificates, especially the death certificate, which obviously is the last existing document and therefore contains the most information. You can send to your local Births, Deaths and Marriages Registry if the death was local, or to the Wellington and Auckland office who keep records for every area in New Zealand. For a small cost you will receive a photocopy.

- The information you get on a death certificate (where it is known) is:

  Date and place of death.

  Full name, sex and age.

  Occupation.

  Cause of death and duration of illness where appropriate.

  Parents' full names including mother's maiden name and father's occupation.

  When and where buried.

  Name and religion of minister who attended the funeral which is a good guide to the religion of the deceased.

  Place of birth and how long they lived in New Zealand.

  Where, at what age and to whom they were married.

  Children living at time of death with their age and sex.

- From this information you can then work backwards. Using the parents' or the children's names you can find their death index, send for their death certificates, get more names and keep going back.

In the making of *Epitaph* the information on death certificates was very useful, especially since our starting point was nearly always a death. In the case of Bobby Leach, discovering that his cause of death was listed as sarcoma of the femur made his slip on the orange peel a little less ignominious. This is not to underplay the value of birth or marriage certificates — it was an Australian marriage certificate that provided the surprising information that Marion Hamilton and Thomas Priestley married some 23 years after Hugh Hamilton's death and that Thomas Priestley had changed his name to Thomas Cullane.

Cemetery transcripts were also a great help to us. Virtually every inscription on every headstone in every cemetery in New Zealand has been transcribed onto microfiche by the New Zealand Society of Genealogists. This information can be found at most of the same places as the Births, Deaths and Marriages Indexes, and sometimes includes details from the cemetery burial record book. These registers are available for inspection at most cemeteries and tell you the date of burial, who bought the plot, how much they paid for it, and occasionally contain a comment from the officiating minister as in the tragic case of Johanna McCarthy, where Father McDonald wrote, "So glad to see my old friend again." In the context of Johanna's suicide, it is a strange comment and leaves us with a mystery.

The cemetery burial register also tells you who the funeral director was, and their records are worth a look, too. In Bobby Leach's case, again, I noted that a carriage was arranged to transport Bobby's wife Sadie to the funeral. It gave the address where the carriage should be sent: hence I learnt where Bobby and Sadie were staying while in Auckland. It's amazing how one piece of information can lead to another.

Death notices in the paper can sometimes give extra information, such as who placed the notice in the paper, or who the family members are.

| | NEW ZEALAND "REGISTRATION OF |

REGISTRAR'S RETURN OF ALL ENTRIES OF DEATHS IN THE DISTRICT OF *Buller*

No.	DESCRIPTION OF DECEASED.			CAUSE OF DEATH.	PARENTS.	IF
	When and where died.	1. Name and Surname. 2. Rank, Profession, or Occupation.	Sex and Age.	1. Cause of Death. 2. Duration of last Illness. 3. Medical Attendant by whom certified. 4. When he last saw Deceased.	1. Name and Surname of Father. 2. Name and, if known, Maiden Surname of Mother. 3. Rank or Profession of Father.	
64	1908. 14 October Westport	Anders Anderson Mariner	M 71 31	Epilepsy 4 days Syncope Guy Hallwright 14 October 1908	Anders Anderson Selina Albertina Anderson formerly Jansen Master Mariner	1908 October 11

The death certificate of Anders Andersen

Best of all, contact your local genealogist group. They can offer you a lot of good advice and shortcuts to save you time. The New Zealand Society of Genealogists puts out a regular booklet full of good tips, and networking with people who have the same surname as you is another way to save time and effort.

Skeletons in the closet

Family history is one thing, but uncovering some significant character or event is another. In the episode of *Epitaph* called 'Finnegan', not included in this book, Catherine Curry was an example of someone compiling her family tree who discovered a lot more than she bargained for. Four of her ancestors had been wiped out in a grisly mass murder. Like us she was able to reconstruct a vivid picture of this incident using many of the excellent archival resources that (for a small fee sometimes) are available to the public.

Newspaper archives are a brilliant resource in this respect. Yesterday's newspapers are what we often think of as just fish-and-chip wrapping; but to researchers of the future, despite TV news coverage, I suspect they will still provide the most comprehensive account of our times. For our recent history, at least, they are invaluable. Murders and trials were covered extensively. Reports on trials were almost as extensive as the court transcripts, plus they included background information on the major characters, often written in wonderfully descriptive language. One of my favourite examples of this is: "The police were forced to act when Dame Rumour with her hundred tongues became busy with the case."

Different libraries and museums around New Zealand hold the old local papers for that area. Microfilms of these can also be interloaned to your local library.